W9-AJS-570
3 4028 06116 2161
HARRIS COUNTY PUBLIC LIBRARY

BAPTIST AND METHODIST FAITHS *in* AMERICA

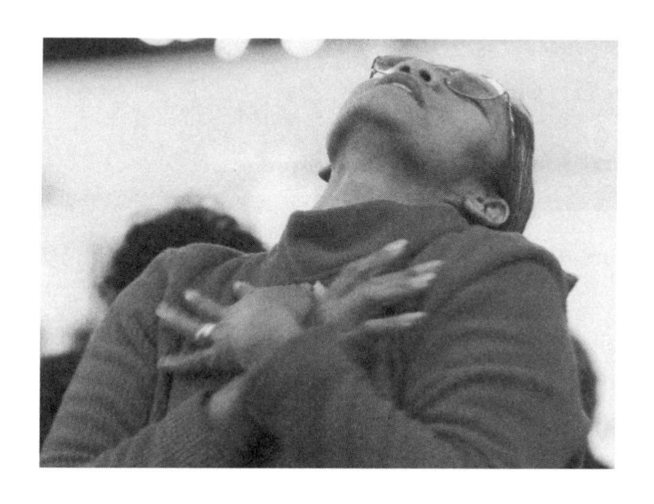

JULIE INGERSOLL

J. GORDON MELTON, SERIES EDITOR

Facts On File, Inc.

BAPTIST AND METHODIST FAITHS IN AMERICA
Faith in America

Facts On File, Inc.
132 West 31st Street
New York NY 10001

Library of Congress Cataloging-in-Publication Data

Ingersoll, Julie
Baptist and Methodist Faiths in America / Julie Ingersoll
p. cm. — (Faith in America)
Includes bibliographical references and index.
ISBN 0-8160-4992-0
1. Baptists—United States—History. 2. Methodist Church—United States—History.
I. Title. II. Series.

BX6235.I54 2003
286' 0973—dc21 2003040819

Facts On File books are available at special discounts when purchased in bulk quantities for businesses, associations, institutions, or sales promotions. Please call our Special Sales Department in New York at (212) 967-8800 or (800) 322-8755.

You can find Facts On File on the World Wide Web at http://www.factsonfile.com

Produced by the Shoreline Publishing Group LLC
Editorial Director: James Buckley Jr.
Contributing Editor: Beth Adelman
Designed by Thomas Carling, Carling Design, Inc.
Photo research by Laurie Schuh
Index by Nanette Cardon, IRIS

Photo and art credits: Cover: Minister, team (Getty Images); McPherson, Graham (AP/Wide World).
AP/Wide World: 40, 48, 57, 60, 63, 64, 69, 73, 74, 76, 82, 90, 92, 94, 103, 106; Art Resource: 35; Baseball Hall of Fame and Museum: 98; Corbis: 30, 44, 67, 100, 108; Courtesy du Plessis Center/Fuller Theological Seminary, 50; Courtesy Southern Baptist Seminary, 111; Flower Pentecostal Heritage Center, 47; Getty Images, 114; Library of Congress: 6; North Wind Archives: 13, 16, 24;
Stock Montage: 18, 20, 27; Tyndale Publishing, 54 (3).

Printed in the United States of America

VB 10 9 8 7 6 5 4 3 2 1

This book is printed on acid-free paper.

CONTENTS

FOREWORD

AMERICA BEGINS A NEW MILLENNIUM AS ONE OF THE MOST RELIGIOUSLY diverse nations of all time. Nowhere else in the world do so many people—offered a choice free from government influence—identify with such a wide range of religious and spiritual communities. Nowhere else has the human search for meaning been so varied. In America today, there are communities and centers for worship representing all of the world's religions.

The American landscape is dotted with churches, temples, synagogues, and mosques. Zen Buddhist zendos sit next to Pentecostal tabernacles. Hasidic Jews walk the streets with Hindu swamis. Most amazing of all, relatively little conflict has occurred among religions in America. This fact, combined with a high level of tolerance of one another's beliefs and practices, has let America produce people of goodwill ready to try to resolve any tensions that might emerge.

The Faith in America series celebrates America's diverse religious heritage. People of faith and ideals who longed for a better world have created a unique society where freedom of religious expression is a keynote of culture. The freedom that America offers to people of faith means that not only have ancient religions found a home here, but that newer forms of expressing spirituality have also taken root. From huge churches in large cities to small spiritual communities in towns and villages, faith in America has never been stronger. The paths that different religions have taken through American history is just one of the stories readers will find in this series.

Like anything people create, religion is far from perfect. However, its contribution to the culture and its ability to help people are impressive, and these accomplishments will be found in all the books in the series. Meanwhile, awareness and tolerance of the different paths our neighbors take to the spiritual life has become an increasingly important part of citizenship in America.

Today, more than ever, America as a whole puts its faith in freedom—the freedom to believe.

Baptist and Methodist Faiths in America

As the American nation was being formed, the role of Protestant churches (Lutheran, Reformed, Anglican, Presbyterian, and Congregational) as the established Protestant bodies in America was quickly challenged by two new Protestant movements—the Methodists and Baptists. The Baptists emerged in England in opposition to the marriage of church and state by demanding a free church, separated from government interference and composed solely of those adults who committed themselves to Christianity. Thanks in large part to the separation of the church and state in the United States, Baptists had emerged, by the 20th century, as the largest Protestant communion in America.

The Methodists had quite different origins, founded as a revival movement within the Church of England. With no intention of separating, Methodists in America set up an independent Methodist Episcopal Church. Its program for evangelizing the nation made it the first national church of the fledgling country. Since then, Methodists have emerged as second only to the Baptists in size within the Protestant realm.

The emphasis on revivalism and evangelism so central to Baptist and Methodist existence was somewhat tempered by theological changes in the 20th century. Those changes contributed greatly to the rise of the contemporary Evangelical movement. In *Baptist and Methodist Faiths in America*, author Julie Ingersoll makes a bold attempt to link the ongoing story of the revivalist tradition and its recent revitalization as the 21st century begins.

– J. Gordon Melton, series editor

INTRODUCTION

Evangelical Origins, Beliefs, and Practices

THERE ARE TWO DOMINANT STRAINS IN AMERICAN PROTESTANTISM. The more widely written about is the reformed Puritan strain. These Protestants followed a sophisticated, thoughtful faith that was rooted in the Reformation theology of John Calvin and Martin Luther.

In America, the first Puritans settled in New England. They sought to build the kingdom of God on earth, and often blended civil and religious authority in their communities. They did not seek religious freedom in the sense that we now use the phrase. In fact, they sought freedom from England so they could practice their own faith, but in those early days that faith did not include the idea of separation of church and state that was later included in the U.S. Constitution.

This book is about the other strain of Protestant faith, sometimes called the Pietistic tradition, sometimes called the free-church tradition, and later often called the revivalist or Evangelical tradition. These various names will become clearer as we explore these other Protestants. Pietists emphasized a life of piety, or devotion, which was to follow a person's conversion to Christianity. They drew on a straightforward, commonsense reading of the Bible, especially in its ethical and moral teachings. Pietists were much more concerned with religious experience and moral living than with scholarly

The Other Protestants

PIETISM: Pietism is a tradition within Protestantism that emphasizes the need for religious conversion followed by a life of piety or devotion. Pietists taught that the world would be transformed only through the transformation of individual souls—a view that has dominated America since its beginnings.

FREE-CHURCH: This movement aimed to set up churches that were not tied to or controlled by civil authorities or governments, as the Anglican Church was in England. As we will see, Methodists and Baptists were among the "free churches."

REVIVALISM: Protestantism in America, whether Puritan or Pietist, has emphasized the central importance of conversion—sometimes called a "born again experience." As a result, American Protestantism has been characterized by what has been called revivalism. Revivals are church services, often held in distinctly different forms than regular Sunday services, designed to bring about conversions. Some were week-long events for which a whole town would cease normal activities; some were meetings that would last all night; some were held outdoors or even at campgrounds—so that they came to be called camp meetings or tent meetings.

PRECEDING PAGE
Powerful preacher
This 1939 photo shows an unnamed Pentecostal preacher at a church in Cambria, Illinois. The often fiery style of evangelical preachers is one of the signatures of the ongoing movement.

approaches to Christianity. Settling in southern New England and the middle colonies, they had tremendous influence on the developing character of the future states they lived in, lending support to the populist spirit that challenged external sources of authority in favor of individual freedom and individual conscience.

Because Puritanism and Pietism are two ways of approaching religion, they cannot be identified solely with specific denominations. Most American denominations have some members who emphasize thinking or understanding like the Puritans, and others who emphasize feeling like the Pietists, and many who balance the two. There are some Episcopalians who are the former and others who are the latter; the same is true for Baptists. This book is about the Baptist and Methodist denominations that, while having some strains that focus on a reasoned, thoughtful approach to faith, have mainly been home to the more devotional, spirit-oriented, revivalist style of faith.

The many forms of Protestant Christianity can be seen as branches of a single tree. All are part of the same tradition, passed down from Jesus to his followers. However, after the Reformation occurred in the 1600s and 1700s, Christianity split off into many different branches. The Reformation was a movement created in response to what some people felt was corruption in the Catholic Church. A variety of different churches were formed to express beliefs their founders felt were not being properly followed by the Catholic Church. Thus today there are several main branches of Christianity—Catholicism and Protestantism, for instance—and all the Protestant faiths themselves split off into still other branches. This book focuses on those denominations of Protestant Christianity that have, as part of their central focus, placed a high priority on having a personal experience with God.

Basic Christian Beliefs

Baptists and Methodists, and other revivalist Christians, hold to the basic points of historical Christianity. They believe in the Trinity, which is the Christian teaching that God exists as one God in three persons: the Father, Son, and Holy Spirit. They believe that Jesus was born of the Virgin Mary, that he was both fully human and fully divine, that he was crucified because Adam and Eve had sinned in the Garden of Eden and all humans from then on were fallen from grace, which is the state of being connected to God.

Christians believe that after being crucified, Jesus rose from the dead (resurrection), and by doing so, defeated the power death has over all humans. They believe that through faith in Jesus' death and resurrection, humans can be saved from their sinful natures, that baptism is the symbol of having been saved, that those who are Christians should spend time together in fellowship, and that the Bible is God's word to His people.

BAPTISM

This is the ceremony in which a person becomes a part of a Christian community. The ritual differs from denomination to denomination, but most involve water in some way and emphasize a person's "rebirth" into the community of the believers in Christ.

So many Christians have agreed with these beliefs that the various Christian churches have set them out in creeds—concise statements of the key aspects of the faith. Christians who can affirm the creeds are considered orthodox (that is, they believe those things the church authorities have said are essential to be called a Christian). But Christians have often disagreed over what these basic beliefs mean. While all agree that Christians should be baptized, for example, they have often disagreed strongly over how one should be baptized or at what point in a person's life this ritual is appropriate.

Likewise, all Christians believe that the Bible represents God's words, but they don't necessarily agree on what that means. Some Christians say the Bible is a book about ethics, teaching us how to live our lives; others say it is a history book, teaching us about the ways in which God shapes human history; still others say it is a science textbook, telling us about the nature of the universe and the world around us. As we shall see, revivalist Christians hold varying views on some of these issues.

Conversion and Re-Baptism

For both reformed Puritans and Pietists, making a true commitment to God and Jesus is the basis for the Christian life; one needs to "convert" from whatever previous beliefs or connections one had to a life fully committed to God. Pietists believed that even the Puritans were too worldly, that Puritan churches had lapsed morally. They advocated further purification from Puritans and separated from them.

Almost all religions have rituals associated with both recognizing new babies as members of the community and then later marking their coming of age. The Anabaptists, and now Baptists, have "dedications" for infants and baptism for adults, the Puritans have baptism for infants and an affirmation for young adults recognizing their full membership in the community.

While Puritans believe that infants born to church members are considered "children of the covenant" (the covenant is the agreement between God and human beings) and should therefore be baptized, Anabaptists believe that only those old enough to make their own choice to become Christian are really Christian. And therefore, although they might have been baptized by believing parents as infants, they need to be re-baptized once they commit themselves to Christianity. The word "anabaptist" means to re-baptize; Anabaptists, early Baptists, hold freedom of choice in very high esteem.

This emphasis on conversion had great influence on the cultures that emerged in the American colonies, as well. The idea of a moral and religious fresh start in life made sense in a context in which men and women were making a literal fresh start in a new country. This sense of newness and freedom from the past remains a part of the American character. It finds expression in every area of life, from Americans who consider themselves "born again," to the widespread acceptance of psychotherapy (and therefore the belief that people really can change), to business and technological innovation.

Who Were the Puritans?

Puritanism arose as a reform movement in the Church of England and was the form of Christianity the colonists from England brought with them to Massachusetts and to Virginia. Puritans emphasized the religious character of all aspects of life and sought to build a unified community under God, sometimes called a theocracy.

One of the more significant aspects of their impact on America has been called the "Puritan work ethic." Believing that all of life was religious, Puritans considered all work to be a calling from God. Just as ministers were "called by God" to Christian service, Puritans understood farming, blacksmithing, weaving, and every other occupation to be a calling as well. This greatly affected how Americans came to understand work and its role in spiritual life.

The Priesthood of all Believers

Catholicism teaches that priests have the authority to mediate between humans and God. This is based in the belief that humans and God are so far apart that humans can only connect with God through specially gifted people who dedicate themselves to religious lives. These people are called priests.

During the Reformation, those who would later be called Protestants criticized the Catholic church for many things, but this belief that people could not interact directly with God was a central concern. In response, Protestants developed the doctrine known as the "priesthood of all believers." If all believers are "priests" that means they need no human person or institution to go to God on their behalf. This concept also means that all believers have an increased responsibility for the care and community of God's people (the church).

Puritans embraced the priesthood of all believers, but they still had church structures and civil judges who enforced religious laws and obligations. Anabaptists, on the other hand, argued that obedience to the first five of the Ten Commandments, which refer to beliefs rather than actions (see page 12), was between an individual and God and that they should not be legislated by the civil authorities. Puritans called this "antinomianism" which means "against laws," but Pietists and Anabaptists called it freedom of conscience. This part of the Pietist tradition is, in many ways, the root of American freedom of religion and the separation of church and state. The Puritans were very threatened by the level of freedom claimed by the Pietists and especially by the Anabaptists.

Authority and Congregationalism

While Puritans required that those seeking admission to church membership come before the church elders and recount the details of their conversion experiences (to demonstrate that they were indeed truly converted), Anabaptists rejected even this level of church authority. Those who claimed to be converted were believed to be so, those who claimed revelation from God were encouraged to share it, with each believer having the authority to decide for him or herself whether the revelation was truly from God. As believers gathered together for fellowship and to support one another in Christian life, Anabaptists maintained an emphasis on the freedom of the individual.

This emphasis found expression also in the government of free churches. Some churches have an episcopal government, which means that they have bishops and that church authority flows from the top. Other churches are presbyterian, which means that they have an elected board (of "presbyters") that governs them. Anabaptists, those in the free-church tradition, usually have had congregational forms of church government, which means the local congregation retains all authority. The individual believer is largely responsible for himself or herself.

This emphasis also found expression in the separation of church and state. If the individual conscience is sacred, then no one should be compelled to pay taxes to support a religious institution to which he or she does not belong. Baptists were among the first opponents of church establishment (that is, the practice of having an official church funded through tax dollars).

One of the best modern-day American examples of this belief in individual and congregational autonomy is Baptism, whose members still maintain a congregational form of church government. While they organize themselves into national associations, they do so only to work together on shared projects such as evangelism and producing Sunday school materials. The national associations have no control over the decisions made by local congregations. Decisions such as how to spend money, whether to build a new building, and even whom to hire as pastor are decided by a vote of the members of the local congregation. Baptist have also remained staunch defenders of the separation of church and state—although as we will see there is some disagreement among Baptists as to what this means.

THE TEN COMMANDMENTS

From Exodus 20:1-17, these are the Commandments that Moses brought down to the people from Mt. Sinai.

1. I am the Lord your God, you shall have no other Gods before me.

2. You shall not make for yourself a graven image or any likeness of anything that is in heaven [that is, create false idols or gods other than God].

3. You shall not take the name of the Lord in vain.

4. Keep holy the Sabbath Day.

5. Honor your father and your mother.

6. You shall not kill.

7. You shall not commit adultery [have sexual relations with someone other than your husband or wife].

8. You shall not steal.

9. You shall not bear false witness [lie].

10. You shall not covet [inappropriately desire] your neighbor's [possessions].

Perfectionism, John Wesley, and the Methodists

Both strains of American Protestantism have roots in the English Reformation, out of which was formed the Church of England, or Anglicanism. While Puritans broke off from the Anglicanism because they thought it too worldly, John Wesley (1703–1791) launched an effort to reform the church from within. As a student at Oxford University in England, he led a devotional prayer group that focused on sanctification, that is, on seeking holiness.

These reformers developed methods by which Christians could achieve holiness, and thus they became known as Methodists (see the box on page 14). However, in the beginning, they were not a denomination but only a small group of like-minded Anglican Christians.

Wesley came to believe that sanctification referred to the experience in which the Holy Spirit came to live within the heart of a Christian. This was thought to be a separate experience from conversion and was possible for all Christians. After having been converted, Christians were to devote themselves to lives of prayer and piety, seeking sanctifi-

Georgia on his mind
This 19th-century painting imagines Methodist founder John Wesley preaching to Native Americans in what was then the British colony of Georgia.

cation. Sanctification would occur in an instantaneous experience, which Wesley described in his journals as feeling "strangely warmed." Wesley taught that this indwelling of the Holy Spirit empowered Christians to seek and ultimately, through a life-long process, attain perfection.

This Methodist movement within Anglicanism grew from its early days at Oxford and had special appeal in the American colonies. It stayed within Anglicanism until the Revolutionary War—an event that led many colonists to distance themselves from England. The Anglican Methodists in America then became the Methodists, a distinct denomination.

From Calvinism to Arminianism

Both the Baptists and the Methodists developed in the Calvinist tradition. Calvinism, named for John Calvin (1509–1564), the Swiss teacher who developed it, emphasized the nearly impassable gulf between God and fallen humans. Calvinists believe that, after the fall from grace in the Garden of Eden (see page 9), all humans are essentially sinful, or

John Wesley

John Wesley was born in 1703. An Englishman, he had a profound impact on the religion of the American colonies, an impact that survives today as Methodism. Wesley was a devout Anglican (a member of the Church of England). While a student at Oxford University he founded a small group known as the Holy Club. The members of the group met to pray, fast (go without food for holy purposes), and read the New Testament of the Bible in Greek. Their intense devotion and their strict practices (or methods) led to the nickname Methodists.

A friend of evangelist George Whitefield (see page 20), Wesley and his brother Charles Wesley (1707–1788) began preaching in Whitefield's outdoor revival style, although the Wesleys and Whitefields soon parted ways over theological disagreements concerning Calvinism (see page 13). Whitefield was a Calvinist, believing in predestination, and Wesley was increasingly moving toward Arminianism (see below), emphasizing that everyone who seeks God's grace for salvation would receive it (against the Calvinist teaching of divine election).

Wesley was especially drawn to theological writings with a mystical bent, and from them developed the tradition known as Holiness (see page 46). Even with a significant following in America though, Wesley did not intend to separate from the Church of England. Methodism was to be a reform movement within the church. With the Revolutionary War, however, the ties became difficult to maintain and those who followed Wesley's practices in America became a distinct denomination known as Methodist.

"totally depraved," as the Calvinists said. Traditional Calvinists believe that the gulf between God and humans is so great that nothing humans can do can bridge it. In our fallen state, there is no free will, because we are enslaved by our sinful natures; left to ourselves, we will choose evil. Any ability we have to chose good is through God's grace.

Calvinists teach that, although we all deserve to spend eternity in hell, God chooses to save some of us. This choosing for Calvinists is entirely on God's part; we cannot earn it in any way. Christ died for those whom God has chosen and, once chosen, we are as unable to resist God's grace as we were to earn it on our own. And finally, once the all-powerful God has chosen us, there is nothing we can do that would cause us to lose His grace: Once we are saved and destined for heaven, we are always saved, no matter what.

Most Baptists in the American colonies held to some version of Calvinism for a time (we will return to this point later), but Wesley and the Methodists came from a theological system known as Arminianism. Named for Dutch theologian Jacobus Arminius (1560–1609), Arminianism argued for the individual's ability to choose to accept God's grace. For Arminius, God's grace is available to everyone, thanks to Jesus' resurrection. Arminius argued that because Jesus' death made grace available to all, the fall from grace loosened the hold of sin and allowed free will to operate. Those who believe this argued that humans must choose to accept God's grace in order to be saved. The Arminian alteration of Calvinism was to become key to the revivalist tradition in America. While some Calvinists did promote revivalism, revivals made much more sense in the context of Arminianism. Over time most Baptists chose a softer form of Calvinism that made a place for evangelism.

Spreading the Word: Evangelism

With both the Baptists and Methodists agreeing that a person could react to a call to salvation, the job became getting more people to respond to the message of Christ' love for them. The revival tradition was based on evangelism, or the process of getting others to believe as you do.

From the time of the First Great Awakening (see page 18), it became much more important to spread the word about Christian beliefs. Preachers, revival meetings, camp meetings, and other events were held around the country more often as various Baptists and Methodist denominations tried to help their congregations grow by attracting more and more people to accept their faiths.

The spread of the evangelical Christian faiths followed the spread of America westward, as we shall see. Further, the impact of the type of Christianity that calls for its members, as a part of their daily lives, to personally spread the word and recruit new members of the faith, grew over time. Although it has waxed and waned over time, we shall see that in recent decades, the influence of evangelical Christianity has grown significantly, making a mark on nearly every aspect of American life.

1

Early Evangelical Roots in America

THE EARLIEST BRITISH COLONISTS IN AMERICA WERE PURITANS Of one sort or another. Some believed that true Christians needed to separate themselves from those whom they believed to be too worldly. Those colonial congregations broke away from the Church of England. Other Puritans chose to stay within the Church of England and reform (or purify) it. As time went on, the divisions between these two kinds of Puritans grew. One group continued to be called Puritans and the other group took various names, including Baptist.

Baptists were among the earliest settlers in colonial America and many of them advocated separation most strongly. Most notable among these early Baptists was Roger Williams (1603–1683). Williams, a Puritan minister, came to the Massachusetts Bay Colony in 1631. He was invited to become the minister at Boston Church but, since that church had not separated itself from the Church of England, he refused. He criticized the civil leaders in the Massachusetts Colony for their efforts to legislate on issues he saw as tied to freedom of conscience. Eventually, the colony came to see Williams's unusual views as too disruptive and asked him to leave the colony.

Williams left in 1636, and founded the first of the colonies to separate church and state and to guarantee religious freedom: Rhode Island.

Established on land purchased from the Native Americans as a refuge for persons persecuted for their beliefs, Rhode Island would become home to many Baptists.

There was another group of Christians chased out of the Massachusetts Bay Colony by the Puritans, and Williams helped them purchase land from the Native Americans for a colony as well. This group, influenced by the theology of Anne Hutchinson (1591–1643), emphasized radical freedom of conscience and openness to continuing revelation from God.

In the end, the Puritans of the Massachusetts Bay Colony exiled Williams and Hutchinson for being "extremists." But given the long-term impact of these two, and others who agreed with them, it seems important to point out that people who are first called extremists by those in authority often become the leaders of important movements.

PRECEDING PAGE
Religious radical
Former Massachusetts colonist Roger Williams, seen here in a drawing showing him arriving in the New World, later founded Rhode Island as a safe haven for followers of all religions.

The First Great Awakening

Early on, the Puritans dominated much of New England and the Church of England dominated the Southern colonies. The highly motivated

Influential thinker
Massachusetts preacher Jonathan Edwards (1703–1758) was one of the most influential theologians and speakers in early American religion. His writings on the mixing of Protestant faith and the American ideal remain influential today.

Life on the Frontier

The settled communities of the colonies were mostly the home of well-organized, sophisticated faith groups. The American frontier, however, was the home of the more experience-based revivalist religion. To understand this, it helps to begin by looking at which people were most likely to move to the unsettled frontiers, west of the Atlantic Coast. Self-sufficient and independent, the settlers who pushed the borders of the established communities tended to be mostly young, single males. Many were willing to endure the hardship of frontier life because they saw it as better than their options in the settled communities. They may have had few financial prospects, bad reputations for one reason or another, strained relationships with family members or community leaders, or even criminal records. In any case, most were either unhappy or unwelcome in the already settled towns.

At first, the frontiers had no social institutions such as schools or churches—and, unlike the New England Puritan communities, few restrictions on the personal freedom of those who settled there. This environment was very friendly to denominations like the Baptists and Methodist churches. And, as we shall see, aspects of Baptist and Methodist religious life blended well with the character and values of the frontier.

Revivalist religion that emphasized the value of religious experience, the freedom of individual conscience, the independence of local religious communities, and heartfelt conversion, appealed to the simple folks who were living hard lives on the frontier. Highly technical sermons delivered by well-trained elite ministers in established churches were less appealing.

Additionally, the traditions that emphasized the intellectual character of religion placed many requirements on those who would become ministers—and often paid them accordingly. An Anglican, for example, who wished to be a minister had to go to school in England. After years of training, he became a well-regarded citizen with a respected family, a nice home, and a nice church building in which to conduct his ministry. In some of the colonies, this minister could even depend on tax support to pay his salary and the church expenses. None of these benefits was available on the frontier. Frontier settlers could not support such luxuries. So few of the established ministers were willing to go there.

With the Baptists and Methodists, however, religious conviction and a passionate sense of calling were the requirements of ministry—not academic training. This meant that those converted on the frontier in the revival meetings were potential ministers, to lead other converts in the new, tiny, spread-out communities. And, unlike their more educated fellow ministers, the frontier converts had much in common with those simple folks to whom they ministered. Already on the frontier with few of the luxuries of civilization, their services came at very little cost. These hard-working ministers had to support themselves from voluntary contributions. There were, therefore, few institutional limits on the growth of their denominations and lots of motivation on the part of the frontier ministers to make new converts and expand their churches.

first-generation Puritans were replaced by children who had grown up in the church and were therefore less committed. The years of hard work, thrift, and seriousness of the Puritans paid off in terms of wealth but in many ways led the Puritan churches to become more worldly. This process is often called "secularization."

Over time, most religious institutions become secularized (that is, they become wealthier, more status-conscious, more at ease with the world around them.) Because many people look to religion to explain the difficulties in life, secularization is usually accompanied by a decline in the number of church members. New, less secular organizations then develop to meet the needs of those people who are looking for a deeper religious experience. The process is, in that sense, like a circle. The levels of influence of particular religious groups decline but the levels of overall interest in religion seem to stay about the same.

SECULAR

Secular means having to do with worldly concerns and not spiritual ones. It is generally thought of as the opposite of religious. The process of secularization means becoming more interested in things of the world and of "real" life than in things having to do with the spirit or with God.

As the dominant traditions in the colonies became more secular, the traditions that emphasized freedom of conscience and relative autonomy from religious structures began to grow in popularity. A movement that became known as the First Great Awakening began in the mid-1730s, primarily in New England. It was called that because followers felt newly called, awakened, to a deeper connection to God (there would be a Second Great Awakening some 40 years later).

Jonathan Edwards (1703–1758) was pastor of a church in Northampton, Massachusetts, where he began holding revival meetings. Edwards has been considered one of America's best theologians because of the way in which he blended traditional Calvinism with the ideas of personally experiencing religion and an emphasis on emotional conversion. Edwards taught, like all Calvinists, that one could not earn salvation. At the same time, though, he argued that people could prepare their hearts for God's grace and that good preachers could aid in this process. Edwards is famous for his powerful sermons, the most well-known of which is called "Sinners in the Hands of an Angry God."

The person often considered the most powerful preacher in America is George Whitefield (1715–1779). Whitefield first visited from England in 1739, traveling from town to town preaching as a visitor, or what was called an itinerant minister. He preached throughout the colonies from Maine to Georgia. Over the next 30 years he made seven trips though the colonies on tours that each lasted at least a year.

Not everyone appreciated Whitefield's preaching. In fact, he created controversy and turmoil everywhere he went. He often preached that local "worldly" ministers were, in reality, unconverted. And his ministry marks the beginning of a great division in American religion: the division between theological, intellectualized religion and emotional, experiential religion. Neither one of these forms of religion is superior to the other. The more theological traditions produced people who felt close to God and the experiential traditions included many people who were very smart. The division was more a matter of emphasis. However, as we will see, this difference in emphasis had important implications for which traditions would grow.

Call from the pulpit
George Whitefield, shown in this 19th-century drawing preaching to a colonial-era crowd, was the most important of the many revival preachers in the years around the American Revolution.

Some local ministers banned Whitefield from preaching in the pulpits of their churches, perhaps hoping that they could discourage him from preaching in their towns. But he began preaching outside in fields and tens of thousands of people came to hear him do so. And, for Whitefield, fewer ties with local religious leaders meant more freedom to speak in the language of the common people and to criticize the religious elite. This is, perhaps, the origin of the tent revival meetings, held outdoors for large crowds, so common in American churches even today. Many other itinerant ministers followed Whitefield's example, creating a wave of revivalism across the colonies.

This First Great Awakening greatly influenced the identity of the colonies and the people who lived in them. Whitefield used his influence as a devout Christian to raise money to support a charitable orphanage in Georgia. This practice of harnessing heartfelt religion for charity, voluntarism, and social change may have begun with Whitefield, but it became a dominant theme in American religion that persists still.

Franklin on Whitefield

George Whitefield preached in Philadelphia where the American patriot and diplomat Benjamin Franklin, a pointedly non-religious person, would go to hear him just because Whitefield was such a great speaker. Franklin wrote about the experience in his diary, commenting upon the numbers of people who came to hear Whitefield, the amazing distance from which Whitefield's voice could be heard, the clarity of Whitefield's voice, and the preacher's surprising ability to convince even the most skeptical listener (Franklin himself) to contribute funds to a home for orphans in Georgia.

Impact of the First Great Awakening

Perhaps the most significant impact of the Awakening was the creation of a shared national identity among the colonists. Before the First Great Awakening, the colonies were significantly different from one another. No one religious denomination dominated: there were Baptists, Presbyterians, Congregationalists, Anglicans, Quakers, Catholics. There were no official Methodists yet, as the Methodist movement was still part of the Anglican denomination. Some colonies had freedom of religion while others had established churches (that is, churches paid for with public tax dollars). Although Whitefield himself was an Anglican minister, many of his converts in the colonies joined Baptist churches.

The different denominations continued to exist even after the Awakening, but the churches throughout the colonies now had much more in common with each other. The colonists had all been exposed to the revivalist style of religion and there developed widespread emphasis on emotional religious experience, or piety, and suspicion of worldly churches and ministers.

But the impact of the Awakening was broader than its influence on the various Christian denominations. Before the First Great Awakening, the colonists saw themselves as citizens in separate colonies whose political loyalty was to England. Revivalism challenged the existing religious authorities and thus fed American independence and individualism. It emphasized the degree to which people were responsible for their own spiritual state and their relationship with God. It undermined the social status of the religious elite and emphasized a relative equality before God. In playing to the colonists' sense of individualism, equality, and independence, the Awakening challenged the legitimacy of the authority England held over the colonists and produced a national consciousness that was necessary for the American Revolution to take place.

The Second Great Awakening

In America the real coming of age of the revivalist, experiential tradition occurred during the period known as the Second Great Awakening. The Second Awakening was different from the first in several ways. It was far more sweeping, reaching from upstate New York and all through the South. It was theologically different in that much of it was it was Arminian rather than Calvinist. And denominationally it was different in that it was overwhelmingly Baptist and Methodist. In fact, between the Revolutionary War and the Civil War, Baptist and Methodist became the dominant forms of Protestantism in America.

In 1776 more than 36 percent of religious people belonged to the Congregationalist or Episcopalian denominations (both representative of the rationalist, establishment Puritanism) and fewer than 19 percent belonged to either Baptist or Methodist churches. By 1850, though, the picture had changed completely. Only 7.5 percent of religious people were Congregationalist or Episcopalian and nearly 55 percent were either Baptist or Methodist. The story of how this occurred is largely the story of American religion in the 19th century.

The beginning of the Second Great Awakening is commonly associated with a series of revivals in New England towns between 1797 and 1801. These led to revivals at Yale College, where as many as a third of the students were converted. Revivals at Yale and in the New England towns continued in fits and starts well into the middle part of the 19th century.

The New England revivals are often considered just the first stirrings of the major revivals of the Second Great Awakening. No denomination gained more in these revivals than the Methodists. As discussed earlier (page 12), Methodism began as a reform movement within the Anglican Church. With the growing support for the American Revolution came an emphasis on democratic religion and an increasing criticism of hierarchical and distant religious authority. When the colonists began to demand independence from England, they also wanted a church identity in the colonies.

Some stayed loyal to the Anglican Church and came to be called Episcopalians. Others decided to split altogether and form a denomination that was more focused on individual religious experience. Those Anglicans became Methodists. At the turn of the 19th century there were very few of them, but that was about to change dramatically. Methodists formally maintained the church structure of Anglicanism (a hierarchy run by bishops) but for many years the Methodists were growing so quickly on the frontier that they effectively had a much more democratic church government—which in turn made integrating new members much easier.

Gone camping
This late 19th-century drawing shows a camp meeting from the 1840s in upstate New York. Notice the tents in the background where attendees could rest, eat, and pray.

Camp Meetings Are Born

In 1800 and 1801, camp meetings at the Gasper River Church and at Cane Ridge, Kentucky, became an important form of rural revivalism. Known for their emotionalism, these meetings sometimes lasted weeks or longer and attracted tens of thousands of people. Witnesses recounted physical demonstrations of religious experiences that included falling down, screaming, "jerking," dancing, barking, laughing, and running. While these behaviors may seem unusual, it is worth noting that such practices exist in most religions and continue today in many forms of Christianity. However, even at the time a gap had already developed between elite intellectual religion and popular experiential religion, which made such practices very controversial. One of the biggest supporters of camp meetings was Methodist bishop Francis Asbury (1745–1816)—who defended these practices (or "exercises," as they were called), which many saw as crude and excessively emotional.

Camp meetings were held outdoors and people came from all over to camp, meet other people, and experience religious revival. Originally used as a revival technique by Baptists, Methodists, and Presbyterians, camp meetings eventually became most closely identified with the Methodists. Many Methodist camp meeting facilities still exist throughout the mid-Atlantic region and the South. They were first set up informally with tents. Later, and as people returned year after year, more permanent cottages were erected at camp meeting sites.

Over time, the camp meetings evolved from seemingly out-of-control, emotional revivals with very little structure, to settled establishments with cottages, governing boards, and families that came year after year for a vacation that was seen as wholesome and spiritually renewing. This is another example of the process we have called secularization, in which religious organizations are founded in opposition to the settled authorities, grow rapidly, and later decline as they become more worldly and established.

In addition to encouraging people to renew their commitment to their faith, camp meetings also served important social functions. Because farm work was demanding and farm families lived far from one another, socializing was often rare in farming communities. Camp meetings, much like state fairs, provided welcome opportunities for people to come together. When friendships and even marriages developed from camp meetings, those relationships took on a certain character that

The Circuit Riders

Another innovation in religious practice that developed during the Second Great Awakening was the circuit riding preacher. Methodist ministers were known for traveling from one town to the next on horseback, preaching to those who would listen, starting up small churches among them, and then moving on to the next town and doing the same thing.

Circuit riders preached a simple, direct faith, in the straightforward language of rural people. They played down theological issues and advocated, instead, that Christians should focus on devotion to God and the condition of their hearts.

Unlike earlier itinerant ministers, the circuit riders returned season after season, year after year, bringing revitalization to the new churches, along with books and news of the region. Once again, Methodists were on the cutting edge of bringing religion to the people. The established New England ministers did not wish to endure the hardships that the circuit riders welcomed. Consequently, the number of Methodists grew (by the middle of the 19th century Methodists were the biggest Protestant denomination), while the numbers of Congregationalists and Episcopalians declined.

A significant factor in the growth of Methodism was its willingness and ability to go to where the people were—without regard for existing support structures. Once people were converted, though, Methodists were able to capitalize on their numbers because their structure allowed them to recruit ministers from the common people and therefore establish new churches. The ministers connected well with the people, and in turn attracted new members, leading to further growth.

was tied up with religion. In early 19th century rural America attending camp meetings became a popular American cultural ritual.

Charles Finney's Important Role

If George Whitefield was the architect of the First Great Awakening, Charles Grandison Finney (1792–1875) was the central figure in the Second Great Awakening. From 1825 to 1830 Finney conducted a series of revivals in upstate New York. His training as a lawyer served him well as a preacher and listeners remarked that his sermons sounded like a lawyer arguing a case rather than a minister preaching a sermon. This suited Finney fine because he believed it was traditional religion that kept people from experiencing real Christian conversion.

Finney was controversial from the start, arguing that revivals be organized by anyone with the right techniques; deep spirituality was not essential. Finney published his techniques in a manual called *The New Measures*. These measures included what Finney called "protracted meetings." According to Finney, religion became routine when it was predictable and tied to a structured time frame. Revivals could be created, in part, by moving the religious meetings from their regular Sunday morning schedules. Revivals would be during the week and would last for hours on end.

Finney also allowed women to make exhortations (or public pronouncements). He spoke in tough, forthright terms—often confronting sinners directly and by name. He advocated the use of what he called an

Revivalist
Charles Finney was a key figure in the revival movement in the 1820s. His style and teachings became popular and were often imitated, helping spread evangelical fervor even further.

"anxious bench," a place in the front of the sanctuary where sinners could come to inquire about salvation, receive prayer, and even public confrontation for their sins. Finney also made use of modern promotional techniques; "selling" religion, if you will. He developed a team approach to revivalism whereby supporters would arrive before him, making arrangements and generating interest in his upcoming arrival. This technique was controversial, in part because Finney's supporters did not seek the approval, and work through, the ministers in town.

Finney departed significantly from the dominant Protestant theological views. Whereas the New England Calvinists, and therefore the First Great Awakening, had emphasized the view that humans were trapped in original sin with no ability to choose salvation on their own, Finney argued that sin was not an aspect of human nature but a voluntary act that was avoidable. He believed that humans had the option of choosing salvation and holiness. For Finney, real salvation was evident in the saved. A truly converted Christian would choose to avoid sin and worldly pleasures, and demonstrate his or her new commitment to faith with social action.

Unlike the Methodist revivals of the rural South, Finney's revivals were primarily urban. The area in upstate New York where he preached many revival meetings became known as the "burned over district," a reference to the repeated revivals he created. As a region infused with religious fervor, the burned over district became the birthplace of many American religious movements, including the Mormons (Church of Jesus Christ of Latter-day Saints).

The African-American Evangelical Experience

So far we have focused on Evangelical Protestant revival movements that were dominated at least in pre-Civil War America, by white Christians. Experiential religion and revivalism were also important factors in the development and growth of African-American Baptist and Methodists churches—which make up almost all of what has become known as the Black Church in America.

From the beginnings of slavery in the American colonies, there were questions about the relationship of Christian conversion to slavery. The Quakers argued that Christians could not own slaves and from 1776 onward refused church membership to slave holders. Many white Christians in other denominations also believed that there were deep problems associated with ownership of a Christian brother or sister, and argued that slaves who became Christians had to be freed. For this reason, many slave owners prohibited missionary activity among slaves. Where missionary activity was allowed it was often strictly controlled so that the readings of the Bible would serve to keep slaves submissive to their owners. In the slave quarters, however, slaves maintained religious practices brought with them from Africa, adopted various practices from Christianity, and made religious innovations related to their new surroundings.

Early on, many of the Baptists and Methodists opposed slavery; but as they realized that their support for abolition closed off their access to slaves, they often abandoned that principle. By assuring slave masters that conversion would make their slaves more honest and more obedient, Baptist and Methodist preachers were allowed to preach to slaves. Their plain spoken, direct manner was as easily adapted to the conversion of slaves as it was to frontiersmen and women.

While some slaves who joined established churches looked to the next life to be free, many found in Christianity justifications for resistance and even insurrection. God's promises to lead Israel out of bondage provided especially meaningful examples for those who opposed the institution of slavery. By the 1820s there were thousands of black members of "white" Baptist and Methodist churches, although activities in these churches were often segregated by race.

Initially, segregation seemed to give African-Americans more autonomy. In integrated churches, black members were under the direct control of whites because church leadership positions were always held by whites. Segregated churches were also set up by whites and controlled by whites, but gave immediate day-to-day autonomy to blacks, who elected their own leaders and chose their own ministers.

AN IMPORTANT LEADER

Richard Allen (1760–1831) was the first bishop of the African Methodist Episcopal Church and founder of the first black Christian denomination. As a slave, he was converted by a Methodist circuit rider. Having purchased his freedom in 1783, he himself became a traveling preacher. In Philadelphia he concluded that too many Blacks found the existing churches unacceptable because of the ways they were kept subordinate by whites. He subsequently established the first denomination for African Americans.

God and the Civil War

Much as the First Great Awakening produced factors that made the Revolutionary War possible, the Second Great Awakening can be said to have contributed to the development of the split that led to the Civil War. Of course, the rise of the Black Church and its criticism of slavery were important factors.

The anti-elitism of the Awakening lent itself well to the opposition to slavery. Revivalism taught that true Christians did not place

A place of their own
This drawing from 1870 shows African Americans freely worshiping in a church of their own. Separate Black Churches continue to be a big part of the Baptist community.

emphasis on worldly considerations of class, gender, social position, and race but, instead, on righteousness based on devotion, piety, and morality. A person's status was to be determined by his or her relationship with God rather than by external characteristics. The growing numbers of slaves who converted and joined Black Churches led white Christians to become increasingly uncomfortable with the persistence of slavery as well. It became increasingly difficult to defend the enslavement of Christian brothers and sisters.

The Second Awakening also produced social changes that were necessary for the war to occur, the most important of which was the development of distinct regional identities. The Awakening in the North was set in the cities. Leaders insisted that those converted become active in social reform, which for many meant working for the abolition of slavery.

Northern revival converts believed, following the Puritan tradition, that the Union was the earthly manifestation of the Kingdom of God. They believed that permitting slavery to continue was a grave sin for which they were also accountable. In addition to believing that they had to purge the Union of the sin of slavery, they also believed that the Union, as the visible Kingdom of God, had to be preserved at all cost. The song *The Battle Hymn of the Republic* exemplifies this clearly, as the Union saw the war between the states as a parallel to the battles associated with the second coming of Jesus and the establishment of the Kingdom of God. (In the Book of Revelations and other places in the Bible, scriptures predict an enormous battle between the forces of good and evil that will occur at the end of the world, at the time of the return of Jesus to establish God's Kingdom.)

The character of the Awakening in the South was distinctly different. Predominantly rural, it arose from a highly ordered society that held to populist agrarian values. The urban North was seen as arrogant and condescending. The cities were seen as rude, filthy places in which people lost their ties to the land and their ties to others. Southerners saw the "Old South" as God's Kingdom.

Early on, Southern converts also criticized the institution of slavery; in fact, they made most of the same arguments that were made in the North. But over time, those criticisms were silenced. In part, as we have mentioned, they were abandoned when preachers saw their opposition to slavery as a barrier to their preaching to slaves. But Southern opposition to slavery also died with the growing regional tensions between the North and the South. As Northern arguments against slavery sounded, to Southerners, increasingly shrill and arrogant, defense of slavery came to be part of Southern patriotism.

The Split Over Slavery

In what some historians have considered the last straw leading to war, Baptists and Methodists split over slavery. In 1836 the Methodists officially opposed the practice of slavery, although at that time they also opposed what was seen as the excesses of the abolitionists. Once the church officially called slavery a sin, the next question was what to do about church leaders who were guilty of the sin of slavery. The stage was set for the divisive meeting in 1844 in which northern and southern delegates fought over governing issues that were seen as representative of a deeper divide, and ultimately split into two distinct bodies: the Northern General Conference and the Methodist Episcopal Church, South. They were not re-united until 1939.

Baptists have a distinctly congregational form of church government (see page 11), so their split took a slightly different form. There was no central body to divide, but Baptists had joined together in associations to support missionary work and other projects. Through the early 1840s the mission board maintained neutrality on the slavery issue.

Tensions between northern and southern state organizations were growing to the point where the Georgia Baptist Convention nominated slaveholder James Reeves as a missionary and his nomination was rejected. When the Alabama Convention asked the mission board to state its formal position concerning support of missionaries who owned slaves, the mission board formally opposed such support. Baptist conventions from slave states organized on May 8, 1845, to form the Southern Baptist Convention and organize their own common projects. Baptists have still not re-united, although in 1995 the Southern Baptist Convention issued a formal proclamation renouncing its earlier support for slavery.

The Awakenings and the Black Church

From the earliest days on this continent, religion was an important influence in the black community. The Africans brought a variety of religious influences with them, ranging from tribal religions to Islam. On the American plantations they encountered Christianity. In many cases, Christianity was used to encourage slaves to be obedient and submissive.

The slaves were often forced to participate in the white plantation owners' churches, but this was just one part of their religious experience. The variety of independent and even secret expressions of religious community among slaves is often called the "invisible institution." When Christianity found expression outside white control, it often provided a language and a vision for freedom. The Hebrew Bible, or Old Testament, played an especially important role in this respect, as the slaves learned the story of Exodus in which God liberates his people from slavery.

Over time there emerged a number of independent Black Churches. Sometimes these independent churches were truly independent, founded and led by free blacks. Other times, however, the independence was relative in that the churches were affiliated with and controlled by white churches and often the pastor was white. But the Black Churches, whether entirely independent or not, were the primary place for blacks to experience an independent community and develop leadership skills that would ultimately have tremendous impact on the American culture in general.

The Awakenings emphasized equality of believers before God, the experience of God through the Holy Spirit that paid no heed to education or status levels, and authenticity over authority. For these reasons the Awakenings were especially appealing to those who were often denied status and power—especially women and African Americans—and led to the growth in the number of independent Black Churches. The African Baptist Church, the African Methodist Episcopal Church (AME) and the African Methodist Episcopal Church Zion (AMEZ) drew both free blacks and fugitive slaves. Well-established in the North before the Civil War, these black denominations made great strides in the South in the period immediately following the war.

Although historians have written about "the Black Church," it is important to point out that this label, to some extent, creates the impression that there is one unified black religious experience in America, which would be a gross misrepresentation. African-American religion is as complex and varied as the religious expression of any other community in America. Furthermore, African Americans can be found among every religious tradition, from Judaism and Islam to Hinduism and Buddhism. (For a wider look at African-American religions, see another book in this series, *African-American Faith in America*, by Larry G. Murphy.)

2

Key Evangelical Beliefs and Events

THE RISE OF EVANGELICAL PROTESTANTISM IN ITS MANY FORMS IN the United States can be traced to a series of key events. Just as important, however, are the beliefs that drove many of those events and inspired many of the key figures. Understanding the underpinnings of belief that have driven this important movement within Christianity is one of the best ways to understand why they have had such a big impact on the United States over the centuries.

Millennialism

American Protestants have always emphasized their belief that history has a purpose, a real direction and a goal, and that this purpose and direction are determined by God. This view has been expressed in a variety of ways in American religion, culture, and history. The earliest Puritans, for example, believed that they were on God's "errand into the wilderness." According to the Puritans, the Kingdom of God began with the resurrection of Jesus; it was now up to believers to continue the work of Jesus in the world. In their view, they were building a community that would be the Kingdom of God on earth, and that New England would be a "city on a hill" that the world could look at to see the evidence of God's hand in history.

PRECEDING PAGE
End of the world?
Folk artist Peter Besharo created this vision of Judgment Day in his 1950 painting To God Be the Glory. *The impending coming of God is one of the key focuses of Evangelical Christians.*

As recently as the first Ronald Reagan administration (1981–1989), this idea of America as a "city on a hill" has been promoted in America. (The phrase was first used in a sermon given by Puritan leader John Winthrop in 1631 aboard the *Arbella*, a ship bringing English Puritans to the American colonies.)

One example of this belief that events were preordained came from a Massachusetts farmer and preacher named William Miller (1782–1849). During a Baptist revival in Vermont, Miller converted and became extremely interested in prophecy as described in the biblical books of Daniel and Revelation. Studying his King James Version of the Bible, he concluded that the prophecies promised Jesus' return to earth in 1843. He became a Baptist minister in 1833, after which he became well known for his lectures on the Second Coming of Christ.

Some historians believe that, by 1843, hundreds of thousands of Christians (many of them Baptists and Methodists) had been influenced by Miller's teaching and believed that the end of the world had come. When Jesus did not return, some of Miller's associates argued that the prophecy was not wrong, but that the calculations contained

Seventh Day Adventists

Following the Great Disappointment in the 1840s, the Adventists continued to expect the immediate second coming of Jesus and joined together to form a denomination that came to be known as the Seventh Day Adventists (advent refers to the expected return, and Seventh Day because they kept the Sabbath on Saturday as the seventh day of the week). Since its beginnings Adventists have been in high tension with the rest of Protestant America, as they believe that their true citizenship is in the Kingdom of God rather than in the nations of this world about to be destroyed. They refuse to vote, serve in the military, or work on the Sabbath (Saturday).

Despite their seemingly non-political character, though, these issues have led to their having a significant influence on American law related to freedom of religion. Through numerous cases that have been decided by the U.S. Supreme Court, Adventists have been responsible for securing freedom of religion for many minority groups.

Like many traditions that cause tension in the general community, Adventists drew new members from poorer, disaffected people. Over time, however, the more settled leaders became more established in the world and less like the disaffected converts. This has produced unresolved tensions and divisions within the Adventists themselves. There are approximately 725,000 Seventh-Day Adventists in the United States.

some minor errors. They revised those calculations twice, proposing two alternate dates. When nothing happened on the date in October, 1844 (now called the "Great Disappointment"), Miller withdrew from the movement. However, his followers later formed several new denominations, the largest being the Seventh-Day Adventist Church.

Is the End Coming?

In the late 19th century, this interest in how God's plan would play itself out in history took an interesting turn. As Baptists and Methodists became prominent denominations, especially through the area now often called the "Bible Belt" in the American South, the theology known as Dispensationalist Premillennialism took hold. This term simply means "end times theology." According to this belief, a terrible period of tribulation characterized by seven years of wars and famine will take place, after which Jesus will return and rescue Christians from experiencing the worst of the tribulation in what is called "the Rapture." End times theology teaches that a great battle between the forces of good and evil, called the Battle of Armageddon, will end with the return of Jesus to set up the Kingdom of God on Earth.

This belief can be traced to 19th century theologian John Nelson Darby (1800–1882). Darby developed a systematic interpretation of the Bible in which God dispensed (thus the term dispensationalist) grace (God's favor or healing power) in different ways in each of seven different periods of history. According to this reading of the Bible, our current period, the "church age," will end with a Great Tribulation, Jesus' return, and the beginning of the Kingdom of God.

This interpretation might have remained obscure had it not been for the work of Cyrus I. Schofield (1843–1921). Schofield produced the first annotated Bible using Darby's ideas in his reference notes. As use of the study Bible became widespread in conservative Protestantism, so did Darby's ideas about how God dispensed grace.

THE BEAST IS COMING?

Here is a short excerpt from the book of Revelation, chapter 13, describing one of the terrors the book says awaits people during the "end times." The book is filled with such vivid descriptions.

And I saw a beast rising out of the sea with 10 horns and seven heads, with 10 diadems [crowns] upon its horns and a blasphemous [anti-God] name upon its heads. And the beast that I saw was like a leopard, its feet were like a bear's, and its mouth was like a lion's mouth. And to it the dragon gave his power and his throne and his great authority. One of its heads seemed to have a mortal wound, but its mortal wound was healed, and the whole earth followed the beast with wonder. Men worshiped the dragon for he had given his authority to the beast, and they worshiped the beast saying, "who is like the beast, and who can fight against it?"

The Rise of Fundamentalism

Once again, the secularization process can be seen as the engine that drives the growth and shapes the character of American religion. This is especially true for the Baptists and Methodists, because, as previously discussed, it was the secularization (worldliness) of the churches in the established communities that enabled the Baptists and

Timing Is Everything

Among people who believe in Millennialist ideas there remains disagreement over the details of the events to come. Each of these views is based in different understandings of what the Bible teaches and each helps Christians see the details of their day-to-day lives as important.

Specifically, there is debate over the timing of the Rapture in relation to the Great Tribulation. Most believers think Christians will not have to endure the entire seven-year period of the Great Tribulation. Jesus will return and rescue Christians from it. Disagreement remains, however, on whether Christians will be rescued before the Tribulation, during the Tribulation, or after the Tribulation. This may seem like insignificant wrangling over unimportant details, but actually, the division between the first group and the second two groups is also often the dividing line between groups that are prone to violence and those that are not.

Groups that do not expect to have to live through the Tribulation are not prone to interpret misunderstandings between themselves and others (the government, for example) as a sign that the period of Tribulation has begun. Groups that expect to be involved in violent confrontation with forces of evil are much more likely to respond to confrontation with violence.

Methodists on the frontier to grow so much more quickly than the other denominations. But the denominations that first benefit from the process of secularization often later become more secular themselves and lose members. This is exactly what happened to the the Methodists in the northern states at the end of the 19th century.

Through most of the 19th century American Protestantism was revivalist Protestantism. But by the late 19th and early 20th centuries there was a series of cultural developments that fed the process of secularization in the Protestant denominations, dividing them into two groups that are often called Fundamentalist and Modernist.

Fundamentalists and Modernists divide over one essential question: What is the relationship between religion and culture? Fundamentalists believe that religion is unchanging; that truth was given at some previous point in history; that it exists on its own, independent of culture; that it stays the same forever; and that culture must be shaped to meet the demands of truth. Modernists believe truth evolves over time in the context of culture. Modernists believe religion needs to change over time to meet the changing demands of a changing culture. These two orientations produced two distinctly different groups, the conservative Fundamentalists and the more liberal Modernists.

Fundamentalism arose at the beginning of the 20th century in response to the challenges of Modernism, which was growing in influence. Fundamentalism found a home in many Baptist churches, but it can certainly be found in many other denominations as well. Concerned about Modernist interpretations of the Bible, Fundamentalist Christians from the revivalist traditions emphasized what they called the fundamentals of the faith, thus their name.

Many of the leaders of this movement helped produce a series of pamphlets called *The Fundamentals*, defending a literal reading of the Bible against a historical reading of the Bible, as practiced by Biblical scholars of the time. Between 1910 and 1915, the Stewarts, a successful family who owned Union Oil, paid to have the 12-volume series distributed to pastors, church leaders, and Bible teachers free of charge. In all, 3 million copies were distributed worldwide. *The Fundamentals* argued that such points as the virgin birth of Jesus; the miracles described in the Old and New Testaments; the crucifixion, death, and resurrection of Jesus; as well as his eventual return in the manner expected by those believing in the end times, were all literally true and should be believed as literally true by anyone claiming to be a Christian.

The Fundamentals launched the conflict between those who would bring science to bear on their interpretation of the Bible and those who believe that the Bible needs no interpretation—a conflict that continues today.

The cultural developments that produced this division include scientific developments, developments in Biblical scholarship and religion, and the economic and social transformation of the Industrial Revolution. Insofar as Baptists and Methodists resisted those developments, they continued to grow. But as they were influenced by those developments, reform movements within these denominations gained members.

Evolution and the Scopes Monkey Trial

In the first few years after Charles Darwin's *Origin of Species* was published in 1859, most American attention was focused on the Civil War and the Reconstruction period immediately following the war. Very little attention was paid to the new theory of evolution Darwin offered.

Some Christian leaders and theologians who would eventually be identified with the Fundamentalist movement had little problem with evolution as a theory. As they saw it, evolution did not mean that

DARWIN'S THEORY

According to Darwin's theory, species evolved through a process he called "natural selection." According to the this theory, organisms mutate (that is, they produce offspring with slight differences from themselves). Occasionally those mutations give the offspring advantages over other similar organisms, making them stronger, enabling them to outlive the others and to produce their own offspring with the same advantages, thus improving the species. In other words, just by chance some members of a species might be born with longer legs. Those legs would led them better outrun predators and so they would live longer and produce more of their species with long legs.

God was not the Creator. It could be merely the process by which God created. Eventually, though, evolution came to be seen by Fundamentalists as a tremendous challenge to traditional Christian understandings of human origins and to human values. Not only did it differ from a literal reading of the Biblical book of Genesis, it also depicted the universe as a harsh war of all against all. If natural selection (see the box on page 39) made a species stronger, then efforts to help the poor and the weak could sometimes be seen as harmful to the human species in the long run. As we shall see, views on the theory of evolution became a clear dividing line between Fundamentalists and Modernists and the rising opposition to evolution corresponded with the rise of the Fundamentalist movement.

In 1925 there was a very public confrontation between Fundamentalists and Modernists in the form of a court battle. The state of Tennessee had made it illegal to teach evolution in public schools. A high school biology teacher named John Scopes (1900–1970), with the help of the American Civil Liberties Union (ACLU), challenged the law by deliberately and openly teaching evolution. As expected, he was arrested and the trial that took place became something of a circus.

Two of the nation's most well-known lawyers, William Jennings Bryan (1860–1925) for the prosecution and against evolution, and

Legal opponents
Clarence Darrow (left) and William Jennings Bryan are shown here during a break in the 1925 Scopes Monkey Trial, a key event in the history of Fundamentalism and the debate over evolution vs. creation.

Two Titans

Clarence Darrow (1857–1938) was the son of an Ohio furniture maker. In 1925, at the time of the Scopes trial, he was 70 years old and had become America's most famous defense lawyer. Darrow started his law career as a corporate attorney for the Chicago and North Western Railway. But at age 37 he gave up his corporate practice to defend criminal cases. His clients included murderers, Communists, Socialists, and anarchists.

Darrow was a sophisticated attorney, and in his courtroom arguments he quoted literature, poetry, psychology, and philosophy. He gained a reputation for being intolerant of intolerance, and he volunteered to defend John Scopes. Scopes was the only client Darrow ever represented at no charge.

William Jennings Bryan (1860–1925) became the nation's most prominent figure in the Fundamentalist crusade against the theory of evolution. In public speeches and published writing, Bryan attacked what he called "ape-ism." Bryan believed teachers of evolution should be driven out of public universities, because they were opposed to the Christian religion. At one time, he offered $100 in cash to anyone who signed an agreement declaring that he or she personally was descended from an ape.

By 1925, Bryan had run for president three time and lost. However, he had been instrumental in passage of the Income Tax Amendment (16th) and the Prohibition Amendment (18th) to the U.S. Constitution, and was hoping to add an anti-evolution amendment to his list of accomplishments.

Six days after the Scopes trial ended, Bryan had a huge dinner in Dayton, Ohio, and lay down for a nap. He died in his sleep.

Clarence Darrow (1857–1938), for the defense and against the Biblical account of creation, faced off in the courtroom for eight days. The whole event was covered extensively by the media, but writer H.L. Mencken (1880–1956) was perhaps the most influential reporter. Mencken had such disdain for Fundamentalists that his reporting led the nation to see them as ignorant country bumpkins. Scopes was convicted and fined the minimum $100. The Fundamentalists had won the court case. However, in large measure thanks to Mencken, they had lost whatever cultural clout they had previously held.

Biblical Criticism and Comparative Religions

This period also saw developments in the study of the Bible and religion that challenged the revivalist tradition and gave rise to Modernist religion. Bible scholars explored new ways of studying the Bible called Biblical criticism. It is important to realize that the term "criticism," used in this way, does not mean to criticize the Bible. In this context, it refers to critical thinking, which means to look at something analytically, logically, and thoroughly.

Instead of only looking to the Bible as God's revelation, Biblical criticism looks at it as a historical document. Much as constitutional scholars might study the history of the U.S. Constitution, thinking about which of the founders might have written which part, and how debates about the Constitution produced certain compromises, Biblical scholars explore how the books of the Bible came to be collected together as a sacred text. Who decided which books to include? On what basis did they choose? What was gained and what was lost in such decisions? These questions were challenging to revivalist Christians, who were content with their interpretation of the Bible as the faith originally given to the authors of the Bible.

There was a second development in the study of religion that contributed to the secularization of the Modernist churches as well; this was the comparative study of religion. As long as Christianity was studied as the sole truth and other religions were studied by Christians only so that they might convert their members, the study of world religions served to support revivalist Christians claims to unique truth. But with the growing interest in comparative religions at the turn of the 20th century, Modernist notions about perceptions of truth as part of culture gained support.

Comparative religion, as a discipline, seeks to study the world's religious traditions from a religiously neutral position, but to do so requires that the scholar not claim any unique access to truth from his or her own religious tradition. As scholars of comparative religions found creation stories in the various world religions that seem to borrow from one another, and as they came to see different religions functioning in similar ways in different cultures, it was increasingly difficult to maintain the claim that Christianity is "true" while the other religions are "false."

This view was not a serious challenge to Modernism. If, as Modernists believe, religion should change to meet the changing cultural needs, then it is fairly easy to re-shape Christianity to account for the discoveries of comparative religion. Fundamentalists, on the other hand, had a harder time, since their belief in an unchanging eternal truth as revealed in the Bible prevented them from making such changes or adaptations.

Revivalist Christians often say that Modernist religion (informed by biblical criticism and comparative religions) "does not preach well," meaning that commonsense readings of the Bible are more effective than complex scholarly interpretations.

The process of secularization shows us that, on this point, the revivalists were right. Since people look to religion to answer fundamental questions of meaning and purpose, for most people the revivalists made the Bible accessible and presented a concrete, literal reading of it. Revivalist churches grew and the numbers of members in Modernist churches that embraced Biblical criticism and comparative religion, thus becoming more worldly, declined.

Believing the Bible

Fundamentalism was a movement that included many Baptists and Methodists, but also conservative believers from denominations opposed to the Modernist impact on religion. Some Fundamentalist leaders tried to propose new doctrines of the Bible's infallibility (correctness on matters of faith and morals) and its inerrancy (correctness on matters of history and science). They also brought forth the need to understand the biblical text as literally true.

Throughout the 19th century, conservative Christians argued for the unique authority and inspiration of the Bible (as described at the 1895 Niagara [New York] Bible Conference). Early in the 20th century, they began to argue that the Bible was infallible and inerrant and that every word was inspired by God. Fundamentalists saw the Bible under attack from Modernists who pointed to what might be contradictions and inconsistencies. To Fundamentalists, the Bible is without error.

The idea of the Bible's inerrancy is often connected with teachings about literal interpretation of the Bible. In fact, many Fundamentalists do not see any distinction between that and inerrancy, and end up claiming that their own interpretation—which they believe to be literal and the only possible one—is also without error. Others, though, recognize that a purely literal interpretation of the Bible is impossible. (For example, Jesus says "upon this Rock I will build my church." Most Christians take this to mean that the apostle Peter will be the foundation of the church, rather than that he was physically turned into a rock.) There is always an interpretation process, in which believers decide which verses are literal and which are not. However,

More than just school
This 1940 photo shows children at a Sunday school run by Baptist minister George Winniman. Along with attending school, needy students received a hot meal.

Fundamentalists have turned believing in the Bible totally and literally into badges of membership in their community.

Sunday Schools, Bible Schools, and Other Christian Youth Organizations

Traditions that make conversion the center of faith face complex problems with incorporating second-generation members into their communities. If one becomes a member by renouncing one's past and making a fresh start as "born again," then how are children raised in the community to become real adult members? They cannot renounce their past within the community. Must they leave for a time and embrace the temptations of the world? Or can they be raised in such a way that conversion is different for them?

Because Christians are centrally concerned with passing their faith on to their children, they have been active innovators in youth ministry. From the rise of the Sunday School Movement in the 19th century to the 20th century youth camps and youth missions such as Young Life, Evangelicals and Fundamentalists have made tremendous investment in these efforts.

The Sunday School Movement actually began in English Methodism in the late 18th century. It was brought to the United States and spread by the Methodist circuit riding preachers. Baptists shaped the movement as they formed associations to produce uniform Sunday school materials. By the turn of the 20th century, Sunday schools drew an estimated 15 million people. The Sunday schools became not only a way to ensure that church members' children would be solidly grounded in the faith community, but also a tool for evangelism as children of non-church members were recruited to attend.

Perhaps no institution has had more impact in shaping the character of conservative Protestantism than the Bible schools. Many have argued that as Fundamentalists lost ground in the Fundamentalist-Modernist controversy, they withdrew from the larger culture and focused on preserving their own culture. Bible schools developed at just this time (the late 19th, early 20th centuries) and served this purpose well.

Fundamentalists believed that seminary-trained ministers were far too likely to have been exposed to, and have embraced, liberalism in the form of Biblical criticism, and that an alternative form of education was necessary to train Christian leaders. Moody Bible Institute in Chicago was one of the first and, ultimately, most influential Bible schools. Founded in 1886, Moody students learned Bible study methods

Christians on Campus

Youth ministries such as Young Life, Campus Crusade for Christ, Intervarsity Christian Fellowship, Teen Challenge and Youth for Christ have been important as ministries to the young and they have also been influential in ensuring that conservative Protestantism maintains its commitment to innovation and cultural relevance.

These groups are often organized as club meetings in churches, schools, and people's homes, and sometimes sponsor widely attended rallies and Christian rock concerts. They criticize formalized religion as not sufficiently relevant to youth and encourage young people to "Christianize" aspects of popular culture, including clothing styles, music, and even slang.

Young Life was founded in 1938 by Jim Rayburn at Dallas Theological Seminary and today has more than 1,000 full-time staff members worldwide. Significantly larger than Young Life, Campus Crusade was founded on a secular university campus—University of California, Los Angeles—in 1951, by Fuller Seminary graduate Bill Bright (b.1921). Campus Crusade has more than 14,000 full-time workers. Founded in 1958, Teen Challenge targets inner-city high school students who face pressures from drugs and gangs.

and evangelistic techniques with the goal of someday serving the Christian community in a full-time capacity. Graduates, both men and women, became ministers, evangelists, missionaries, music ministers, and Sunday school teachers.

SNAKE HANDLERS

One of the more colorful examples of Holiness traditions is the snake handling churches in Appalachia. Taking as their central text verses at the end of the book of Mark ("these things shall follow them that believe—they shall pick up deadly serpents"), these Holiness Christians still make handling rattlesnakes a central part of their worship, believing that they are being obedient to God—more so than Christians who do not handle snakes.

Snake handling, which often means picking up and holding dangerous snakes, in these coal-mining communities serves important social functions. The practice creates a strong sense connection among the people. People are, not infrequently, bitten by the poisonous snakes, and occasionally they die. When someone is bitten the whole community keeps a vigil at his or her house until he or she recovers or dies. The practice also keeps people constantly aware of the reality that life is short and that they could be called to account for their lives at any moment.

Secularization and the Rise of Holiness

The secularization process we have discussed leads us to look for examples of increasing worldliness, followed by decline in membership numbers, and then the rise of revitalization movements that are less worldly. The rise of the Holiness Movement within Methodism, and then the development of Pentecostalism within the Holiness Movement, are good examples of this process at work.

By the end of the 19th century, Methodism was showing signs of secularization. There were fewer and fewer circuit riding preachers and Methodist church members lived frugal, devoted lives that brought them increasing wealth. Those Methodists seeking perfection through the Holy Spirit were growing dissatisfied and started creating new churches that more actively sought to achieve what they called "holiness."

Holiness teachings emphasized purity, devotion, and spirituality. Worldly activities, including drinking dancing, card playing, and theatre attendance, were to be avoided. Holiness also demanded a distinctive personal style that played down the importance of worldly concerns. Modesty was in order, which meant one should refrain from drawing undue attention to oneself. Simple clothing, unstyled long hair, and the absence of makeup and jewelry all indicated that a person's focus was on godliness rather than earthly vanity.

By the 1880s there were a number of independent Holiness churches that included the Church of God and the Salvation Army. By the 1920s there were many more, including the Christian Missionary Alliance (CMA) and the Church of the Nazarene.

The Rise of Pentecostalism

The Holiness churches' emphasis on a person having a deeply spiritual experience of salvation, a process they called sanctification, lent itself nicely to the next revitalization movement, which was called Pentecostalism. The beginnings of this movement date to 1901 when, at Bethel Bible College in Topeka, Kansas, Agnes Ozman (1870–1937) experienced the Holy Spirit in such a way that she began speaking in

Spreading the word
William Seymour was inspired by the Azusa Street Revivals to spread their teachings throughout the Midwest and Texas. The Azusa Street events focused on people experiencing the Holy Spirit.

tongues (which means that she spoke words and made sounds that were not recognizable as any modern language). Her experience was interpreted as a recurrence of the Day of Pentecost written about in the Book of Acts in the New Testament. On that day, according to the New Testament, the apostles of Jesus received the Holy Spirit, which came to them as tongues of flame.

William J. Seymour (1870–1922) heard about this event in Kansas and began spreading word of it through the Midwest and Texas and then on to Los Angeles, where he sparked the Azusa Street Revivals. After only a year of revivals there were nine Pentecostal congregations established in Los Angeles.

The Azusa Street Revivals are noted for being one of the few racially integrated religious events in American history. Seymour himself was African American, and although blacks and whites had often attended services together, it had been unusual for them to share religious leadership. At Azusa Street, leadership was shared between blacks and whites and men and women, at least in the beginning.

Some Pentecostals came to believe that those who had not spoken in tongues were not full Christians. They taught that all the "gifts of the Spirit" mentioned in the New Testament are available to believers. In addition to the ability to speak in tongues, this included miraculous healings, ecstatic experiences with the Holy Spirit that lead to fainting and falling down (being "slain in the spirit"), direct information from God through the Holy Spirit, and other physical manifestations of the Holy Spirit. Many denominations have developed out of this tradition, including the Assemblies of God, the International Church of the Foursquare Gospel, and newer denominations such as the Vineyard Christian Fellowship. In fact, today Pentecostalism is the fastest-growing segment of conservative Protestantism.

Holiness, Pentecostalism, and the Black Church

The Holiness movement among African Americans dates at least as far back as the 1880s in the South. In 1886 the first black Holiness church, the United Holiness Church, was founded in North Carolina. Then in Arkansas in 1889 the founder of the Church of the Living God, William Christian (1856?-1928), argued that the saints of the Bible were really black, a common belief among these Holiness and Pentecostal Christians. Between this period and the origins of what is now called the Pentecostal Movement at the turn of 20th the century, many Holiness

Praying with feeling
This woman, praying at a 2002 Pentecostal camp meeting in Texas, shows the emotional response often seen in Pentecostal or Holiness services.

churches emerged from within African-American Methodism and as splits (or schisms) in black Baptist churches.

In 1893 C. H. Mason (1866–1961) led a Holiness revival in Jackson, Mississippi, that resulted in his being expelled from his Baptist church. He then started what would become the most successful of the African-American Pentecostal denominations. First named the Church of God, Mason soon changed the name to the Church of God in Christ (COGIC) to avoid being confused with a white denomination by the same name. COGIC now claims 13,000 member congregations throughout the world.

In the early days of the Pentecostal movement the revivals emphasized the autonomy of one's experience of the Holy Spirit and the equality of believers. As the movement became more institutional, however, the leadership roles for African Americans (and for women) were more limited. The growth of Pentecostalism and the central role played by African Americans in the early years led to the establishment of several other black Pentecostal denominations.

Black churches often refer to themselves as "Holiness" or "Pentecostal" although the differences between the two today are not distinctly clear, and they are often referred to jointly as "the sanctified movement." This last label comes from the Holiness/Pentecostal belief in a second conversion experience in which the Holy Spirit "sanctifies" (or makes holy) the believer. Both groups emphasize the emotional style of worship that includes speaking in tongues and other spiritual gifts.

Today the black Holiness/Pentecostal churches, like their white counterparts, are divided over the appropriate roles of men and women. Some give complete equality to men and women in church leadership and others reserve the highest positions for men. Still, the Black Churches have provided leadership training and opportunities for men and women. The Mount Sinai Holiness Church of America is such an example. Founded by Ida Robbins in 1923, the church has a significant number of women among its leadership. And even in COGIC, which does not ordain women, they play important leadership roles.

This movement is quite interesting in its approach to biblical interpretation. Black Holiness/Pentecostals also tend toward a literal interpretation of the Bible, but they emphasize the stories of Exodus over the texts emphasized by the white Pentecostals. Wary of white Fundamentalists who used the Bible to justify slavery and racism, black Pentecostals end up with a decidedly less conservative political world view.

3

Evangelical Impact on American Culture

AT THE SAME TIME THAT AMERICAN POPULAR CULTURE OFTEN challenges the values and norms of conservative religion, Evangelical believers are drawn to that culture as a medium for their message. Those who want to share their faith with others see how popular culture lets them do that. Television, radio, movies, and the Internet allow the conservative Christian message to be shared with many more people than ever before. A tricky contradiction comes up, however, because the very interaction that enables conservative Christians to share their type of Christianity with more people also has the potential to change the message they are sharing.

The Developing Evangelical Movement

Through the last decade of the 20th century, the impact of conservative Evangelical Christians has grown significantly. However, to understand how their influence has spread, a little bit of history is in order. As noted earlier, during the 1920s, church members were largely split into two camps, the Modernists and the Fundamentalists. By the 1930s, the Modernists came to dominate most of the larger denominations, including the older Protestant bodies as well as the northern branches of the Methodists and the Baptists. Fundamentalism found its strongest support among Southern

Baptist, Southern Methodist, Pentecostal, Holiness, and recently founded Bible churches.

More liberal, or Modernist, churches developed programs of cooperation that culminated in 1950 in the formation of the National Council of Churches of Christ in the U.S.A. The National Council is the major liberal Protestant organization. By 1950, the Methodists had moved into the liberal Protestant camp. Today, as the United Methodist Church, it identifies fully with the older Protestant bodies. However, many conservative Christians came to believe that modern culture had led Protestants away from essential Christian teachings.

By the beginning of World War II, Fundamentalist Christians faced other problems. For example, they were charged with rejecting the insights of science, sociology, and psychology. They also argued among themselves whether or not to abandon those conservatives who chose to remain affiliated with more liberal Protestant bodies.

PRECEDING PAGE
Big crowd
Charles Fuller was among the first to use radio and television to spread his evangelical message. This 1948 photo shows the Long Beach (California) Municipal Auditorium during a live broadcast of one of Fuller's revival meetings.

By 1940, conservative leaders began to argue for a new form of conservative evangelical faith. This faith welcomed coalitions with like-minded people in all of the churches and favored a new openness to modern culture (for another view, see box on page 53). The great majority of former Fundamentalists favored this new approach. They became known as Evangelicals. In 1942, many came together to form the National Association of Evangelicals (NAE).

The NAE churches moved steadily after World War II to take their place beside the liberal Protestant community in shaping American culture. Their presence is seen in the emergence of Christian bookstores, best-selling books by Evangelical authors, the development of Christian broadcasting, and the popularity of Evangelical Christian entertainers.

End Times Theology and the Popular Imagination

The specific belief among conservative Christians of an impending Judgment Day has spilled out into the larger culture. As discussed in chapter 2, this type of teaching concerns the "end times," the second coming of Jesus, and the establishment of the Kingdom of God on earth. Most Christians believe in some notion of the Kingdom of God, but there are several views as to what this means. The conservative Christian view is that these events will literally take place, following a period of Tribulation and a great battle between good and evil at

Armageddon. The chosen few will be taken away in what is called the Rapture. Another, less literal Christian view, is that the Kingdom of God is a heavenly, spiritual reality, not a literal, earthly one.

In the 1970s there were two expressions of the conservative beliefs that received widespread notice in the larger culture: Hal Lindsay's best-selling book *The Late Great Planet Earth* and the evangelistic film *A Thief in the Night*. Lindsay's book, which sold more than 10 million copies, brought Biblical prophecy to bear on the issues of the day as reported in the newspapers. Rather than attempting to interpret world events, the film *A Thief in the Night* illustrates what life might be like as the end times arrive. Focusing on a group of young people, the film tells the story of the Rapture and Tribulation, the events that directly precede the second coming of Jesus, according to the Bible.

By the end of the 1970s, 40 million Americans claimed to embrace these Bible-inspired views about the end of the world, and these views continued to make their way into popular culture. In 1986, Frank Peretti released the first book in his apocalyptic series *This Present Darkness*. The work also depicted the events of the end times. Peretti's focus, however, was on spiritual warfare in which angels battled demons, with the angels assisted by devoted praying Christians. There have been five more volumes in this series, which has sold 8 million copies.

The influence of books such as these permeated the culture. Pastors cited them in sermons, people talked about them at social gatherings, and the mythical version of events shaped people's perceptions of their day-to-day lives.

The Left Behind Series

None of the popular depictions of end times has had greater appeal than the Left Behind series written by Tim LaHaye and Jerry Jenkins. The first book in this fictional series was published in 1995; the 10th came out in 2002. The novels proceeded from LaHaye's earlier nonfiction work warning Christians of the dangers of secular humanism (including *The Battle for the Mind* and *The Battle for the Public Schools*). We will explore this concern over secular humanism in chapter 5.

LaHaye's work included the view that reality is divided into clearly opposite forces. On the one hand is conservative Christianity, representing "truth"; on the other is humanism, which, in his view, makes humans the measure of all things and is wrong.

Forming Their Own Groups

While some Fundamentalists moved to form coalitions with liberal Christians, more conservative believers dominated the Southern Baptist Convention, the Lutheran Church-Missouri Synod, and all of the Pentecostal and Holiness churches. Their position was strengthened by the many conservatives who left the more liberal Protestant bodies to form new denominations such as the General Association of Regular Baptists (1932) and the Orthodox Presbyterian Church (1936).

Success stories
The best-selling Left Behind series of books features a continuing fictional account of the authors' views of the end of the world, inspired by their Fundamentalist beliefs. The books have spawned movies, web sites, and music, and have also been adapted for younger readers.

For LaHaye, any view that is not in line with his understanding of Biblical Christianity is humanism, and thus wrong.

In the Left Behind series, this theme is explored in terms of the end times. The series details the experiences of those who missed out on the Rapture as they endure the period known as the Great Tribulation. Titles include *The Rise of the Antichrist, Tribulation Force, The Mark: The Beast Rules the World*, and *The Remnant*.

Each of the books in the series has achieved best-seller status, and the 2000 movie (*Left Behind: The Movie*) made from the first novel, starring television star Kirk Cameron, was widely popular among conservative Christians. The Left Behind series has produced a virtual community that now includes a web site, discussion groups, a series of books for younger readers, a newsletter, and a CD of music relating to the series's themes.

The Media and Conservative Religion

There have been longstanding tensions between conservative Christians and the entertainment industry in America. Holiness Christians at one time or another prohibited theater-going and card playing, as well as alcohol use, immodesty, and other activities. Early on, this tendency came primarily from concerns that time spent in worldly activity was not time well spent; that Christians had an obligation to use every waking moment to serve God.

By the 20th century, however, a significant portion of religious conservative political activity had focused on efforts to challenge the content of entertainment, especially in the media. When the film *The Last Temptation of Christ* was released in 1988, conservative Christians—often joined by Catholics—boycotted movie theaters and staged demonstrations in protest of the film's less-than-ideal depiction of Jesus and his final days.

When Southern Baptists came to believe that the Walt Disney Company was undermining traditional family values, both in the practices at its theme parks and the content of its television shows and film, they organized a national boycott of Disney and Disney products. Among the things they objected to was granting equal benefits to the partners of gay and lesbian employees. An arm of the Disney movie business also was producing R-rated movies that included sex and violence, and the Baptist groups objected to these films.

Much of this organized opposition to the media has come from the Reverend Lou Sheldon and his Traditional Values Coalition (TVC). Sheldon's organization extensively monitors television and movies for

Apocalypse Now and Again

It is interesting to note the degree to which apocalyptic visions of the end times have influenced the culture outside the religious community. The word Armageddon, for example, has come to refer not just to the battle depicted in the Bible, but to any potentially devastating violence. And some secular movements, like the environmental movement, are often said to be apocalyptic in nature. That is, they anticipate the ultimate destruction of life as we know it, if we continue on our current path.

Major motion pictures that are not specifically religious in nature have focused on this theme as well. The movies *The Prophecy* (1995) and its two sequels (*Prophecy 2* in 1998 and *Prophecy 3* in 2000), all starring Christopher Walken, are good examples. In the first film, a group of young people finds evidence that the messiah (a Christ figure) has been born and is on earth. As a result, some of them renounce lifestyles they perceive as sinful and others do not. The movie chronicles their efforts to resist the forces of Satan, also known as the "Antichrist."

content it considers offensive to the values his group holds. (Since the last half of the 20th century, conservative Christians have focused on protecting what they call "traditional family values." By this they mean an idealized, usually white, middle-class family, perhaps as depicted on early television shows such as *Leave it to Beaver*. A "traditional family," in the their view, consists of a father who goes to work in business, a mother who stays home as a full-time homemaker, and two to four children.)

ANGELS

The broad-based popularity of angels is attributable, to some degree, to their place in conservative Christianity. The practice of public "witnessing" to the influence of the forces of God in one's life is most common in Pentecostalism, but is also present in Fundamentalism and Evangelicalism. The practice is so common, in fact, that a "testimony time" is part of the regular service at many of these churches. A typical testimony starts with a story about a troubling or even traumatic event, and develops into perceived evidence of God's intervention—often in the form of an angel—to a resolution in which the believer benefits. This practice can be traced to Billy Graham's 1975 book *Angels: God's Secret Agents.*

Angels also play a significant role in Frank Peretti's novels. From their place in conservative Christian imagination, angels made their way into popular culture in movies such as *The Preacher's Wife* and *Michael* and on television series such as *Touched by an Angel.*

Christianity on the Airwaves

In its early years, religious radio broadcasting faced some of the same suspicion from conservative Christians: fear that its worldliness would draw Christians away from serious issues of life and lull them into sin with entertaining programming. At the same time, though, there were religious leaders in the tradition of Charles Finney who were continuously seeking new ways to preach the Gospel to wider and wider audiences. Conservative Christians became highly skilled at using the media to their advantage and, in many cases, they have been innovators who have transformed the media.

By the 1920s radios and radio programming were relatively widespread. Religious leaders (both conservative and more mainstream ones) recognized its potential for evangelism. The widening gulf between the Fundamentalists and Modernists, which we have already discussed, played an important role in the development of religiously oriented media.

Because the airwaves that carry radio programming are considered to be public property, the federal government, in the form of the Federal Communications Commission (FCC), licenses and regulates radio (and now television). Even in its early days, the FCC required a certain amount of free time to be set aside by every station for public service broadcasting—programs that were thought to benefit society. This free time was dominated by the mainline Protestant churches, especially those associated with the Federal Council of Churches, a national group that included representatives from such denominations as Lutheran, Presbyterian, and Episcopal. These mainline churches convinced the major networks to refuse to sell time to Fundamentalist religious broadcasters. In other words, the mainline organizations got the free time and made sure that the Fundamentalists

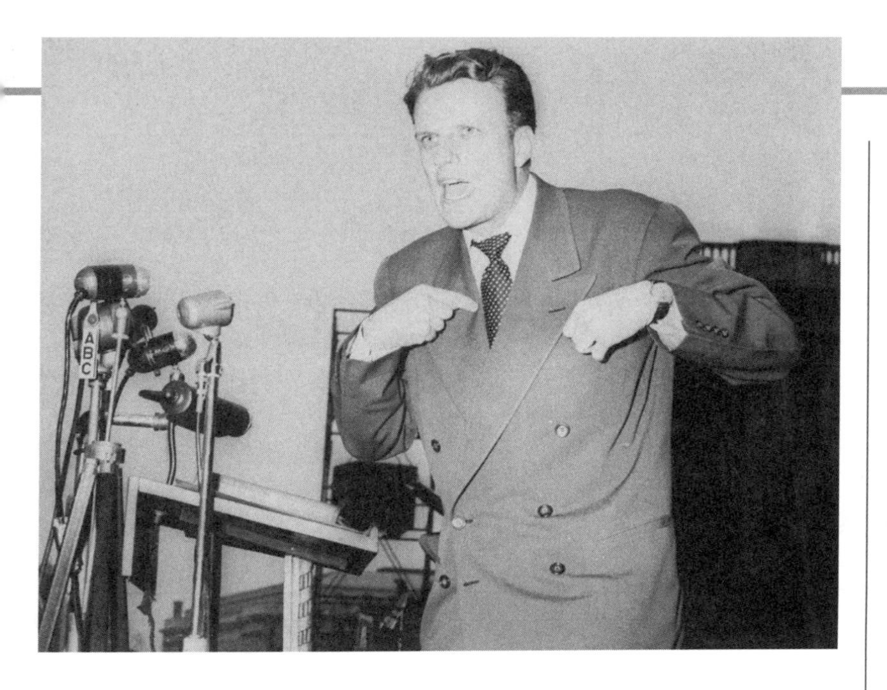

Preeminent preacher
Billy Graham, shown here speaking in front of the U.S. Capitol in 1952, was one of the first nationally-known evangelists. His ongoing revival work has helped him become perhaps America's best-known religious figure in the second half of the 20th century.

were not allowed to buy time on the major stations, and so they dominated the airwaves.

Fundamentalist broadcasters were relegated to small local stations that were more than willing to sell them airtime. As a result, in order to pay for the time on the air the Fundamentalists became very skilled at producing radio shows that would draw an audience who would help pay for the program. The mainline organizations, facing no similar market challenges, did not do as well at fundraising.

In 1924 the National Association of Evangelicals launched the National Religious Broadcasters Association to develop broadcast technology and to protect conservative Christians' access to radio. In 1937 Charles Fuller's *Old Fashioned Revival Hour* took to the airwaves of the Mutual Broadcasting System (one of the first networks to allow conservative radio preachers to buy time) and quickly became a national favorite, airing on 456 stations within five years. It is estimated that by 1944 Fuller had more than 20 million listeners worldwide and received more than 2,000 letters a day.

Fuller became the model for evangelistic use of media. The medium may have been technically advanced for the times but his revival hour was simple and direct in its message. He preached the fundamentals of Christianity in a warm, folksy, manner. His ministry was so successful that it led to the founding of Fuller Theological Seminary,

Syndication Spreads the Word

One of the ways in which conservative religious broadcasters have been innovative is in syndicating their shows. In an effort to respond to being kept off the airwaves, conservative broadcasters began selling their recorded shows to multiple local stations independently in the late 1930s. Such syndication of radio and television shows is, today, the norm.

In another step that anticipated the future of radio, Fundamentalists capitalized on opportunities presented by the development of FM radio. FM was introduced in the 1930s. It had better sound than AM radio, but less power and range. Initially the radio industry was cautious about investing in FM because they were not sure people would switch from AM to FM—especially as a growing television industry was causing the radio market to shrink. The radio preachers saw purchasing FM stations—at a relatively low cost—as a way to have secure access to airways. By the time FM stations became popular, many were owned by Fundamentalist ministries.

In 1960 the regulation tables turned on the mainline Protestant churches as the FCC ruled that networks could take credit for paid religious broadcasting to fulfill their public service time. This effectively froze out the mainline broadcasters, who had relied on free time for their shows and, at the same time, created a huge incentive for those networks that had resisted selling time to Fundamentalists to now do so.

today's largest interdenominational conservative Christian seminary, which has its headquarters in Pasadena, California.

Television: The Big Pulpit

Experience and success in radio broadcasting was easily applied to television broadcasting. Early television evangelists (later often called televangelists) included Oral Roberts (who made his debut in 1948), Percy Crawford (1950), Pentecostal minister Rex Humbard (1953), and Billy Graham (1954). (Jerry Falwell, the Moral Majority Leader whom we will discuss in chapter 5, also got his start as a television minister in 1958 when his Thomas Road Baptist Church services were televised as *The Old Time Gospel Hour*.) These programs became standard television fare from the earliest days of television in America. In 1949 Graham televised the first of his revivals from Los Angeles, a tradition he continued for a half-century.

Television preachers encountered the same opposition as had the earlier radio preachers—efforts by their religious opponents to keep them off the air. But Fundamentalist broadcasters were willing to pay for time to build an audience, as they had done with radio.

Also as with radio programming, the successful shows were those that played down divisive doctrinal issues in favor of heartfelt religious experience and simplicity. In much the same ways as the revivalists of the Great Awakenings were able to attract believers by renouncing the worldliness of the successful ministers, television preachers, too, connected directly with the experiences of common people. The FCC decision that allowed stations to fulfill their public service obligations with paid time had an impact on the television stations as well. The skills conservative television preachers had developed in raising money paid off for the them in the same ways it had paid off for the radio preachers a generation earlier.

While radio and early television programming was mostly limited to broadcasting church services, in the last part of the 20th century much of the religious programming changed to a variety show format. The folksy style of the television preachers blended well with this new format, which also included places for women that had not existed with earlier formats. In 1966, Pat Robertson launched *The 700 Club* in the new talk-show format. Co-hosts Robertson and Jim Bakker conducted interviews, discussed biblical prophecy, and reported on news events. Eventually Bakker left and began his own show (with his wife Tammy Faye as co-host), *The PTL [Praise the Lord] Club*. Robertson's show has included new personalities, including African American broadcaster Ben Kinchlow, and female reporters such as Lisa Ryan and Terry Meeuwsen.

Scandals Slow the Pace

The late 1980s brought hard times for televangelists, as several were tainted by scandals over money and infidelity. The first of the scandals arose when Oral Roberts announced that God had told him He would "call him home" (cause him to die) if he did not raise $8 million dollars for the ministry. To many who were already suspicious of televangelists, this seemed manipulative and self-serving. But criticism over this event faded quickly as stories surfaced about Jim Bakker and his unfaithfulness to his wife Tammy Faye. It quickly became clear that Bakker had not only violated his marriage vows but also used ministry money to cover up his misconduct. Furthermore, the Bakkers had grossly misused ministry money for their own extravagant lifestyle and had been deceptive, unethical, and even illegal in their financial dealings, for which Jim eventually spent time in jail.

Jerry Falwell, seeing the dangers this scandal posed to conservative Christianity in general and to televangelism in particular, tried

Soon the mighty will fall
Tammy Faye and Jim Bakker were among the most successful and wealthy of the televangelists of the 1980s, but a personal and financial scandal brought down their ministry.

to step in and restructure Bakkers' empire but his efforts failed. In the end, this led to an examination of Falwell's own ministry. He was criticized for raising money for one project and using it for others, but the criticism never rose to the level it had of the Bakkers.

In 1988 a scandal involving television preacher Jimmy Swaggart rivaled the Bakker scandal, at least in terms of public notice. Evidence came to light that Swaggart had spent time with a prostitute. In a bold move, the television preacher made a very public tearful confession on television. With lips trembling and tears running down his face, and as his wife and children sat in the audience, he announced "I have sinned." In what seemed like a carefully scripted performance, the cameras cut to his son, who mouthed the words "I love you." The footage of that confession became symbolic of the scandals and the manipulative character of televangelism.

Those outside the world of born-again Christians were suspicious of televangelists from the beginning. However, Swaggart's tearful confession played differently to his followers and other believers. To those Christians who consider themselves born again, repenting of one's sins means, by definition, to be given a fresh start by God. This process is at the very heart of their faith. For that reason, they are likely to give the benefit of the doubt to someone who confesses his or her sins—and many did just that with Swaggart. Although his denomination, the Assemblies of God, removed him from his position, after just a brief time he returned to his ministry without their endorsement but with the endorsement of his followers, who accepted his repentance as real.

Despite the public perception that the televangelists lined their own pockets with contributions (which many of them did), the role of televangelism in the rise of the religious right (discussed in detail in chapter 5) cannot be overplayed. Falwell's television audience was the base from which he launched the Moral Majority in 1979 and Robertson's *700 Club* formed the core of his support for his presidential campaign in 1988, as well as for the establishment of the Christian Coalition, which in 1989 replaced the Moral Majority as the central conservative Christian political organization.

Much like the ways in which the Great Awakenings wove the disconnected colonies into a new nation leading up to the Revolutionary War, and then raised a sense of consciousness before the Civil War, televangelism weaved the conservative Christian community together. Evangelicals and Fundamentalists in Dallas, Texas, were watching the same television preachers and the same Christian news as those in Seattle, Washington. In the end, this meant that they began to identify with one another more closely than they might have otherwise.

Popular Music and Conservative Christianity

There have also been longstanding tensions between the conservative Christian world and the music industry. Initially in the 1960s and 1970s rock 'n' roll was the target. Conservative Christians argued that rock 'n' roll was Satanic music and even insisted that rock 'n' roll albums could be played backwards to reveal hidden Satanic messages. By the 1980s contemporary Christian music had made inroads in the conservative Christian world and, as churches adopted Christian rock as part of their worship services, much of the anti-rock sentiment disappeared. At the same time, however, opposition to heavy metal music and then concern over rap music led to boycotts.

Despite conservative Christian concern about popular music, the rise and influence of contemporary Christian music has had as

From TV to Colleges

An interesting secondary aspect of the televangelist industry is the number of colleges, universities, and seminaries that were founded from the television ministries.

In 1947, Charles Fuller founded Fuller Theological Seminary in Pasadena, California, now the largest interdenominational Christian seminary in the world. Oral Roberts founded Pentecostal Oral Roberts University and a respected medical school in Oklahoma City, Oklahoma, in 1963. Jerry Falwell founded Liberty Baptist College in Lynchburg, Virginia, in 1971, later changing the name to Liberty University. And Pat Robertson founded CBN (Christian Broadcasting Network) University in 1978, which was later renamed Regents University, in Virginia Beach, Virginia.

much influence on the conservative Christian world as any other factor in the 20th century. By the end of the 20th century, the Christian music industry was reportedly worth half a billion dollars. Major artists such as Amy Grant and Faith Hill had crossover hits as Christian music spanned all the genres of secular music from pop and rock to reggae, alternative, heavy metal, and rap.

The impact of music on the baby boomer generation—the people born in the years beginning after World War II—was tremendous. Technology first brought radio and records, and today has brought personal CD players and car stereos. The baby boomers provided a ready market for contemporary Christian music, and churches that sought to reach baby boomers capitalized on their interest in music by using contemporary music in their church services.

Beginning with the Jesus Movement of the 1970s (see chapter 7), Southern California hippies converted to evangelical Christianity. But while they adopted the teachings of conservative Christianity, as a youth movement they rejected many of the trappings of that world. They wore their casual clothes to church, they kept their hair long, they demanded an informal ministry style, and they brought their love for rock music to their new churches.

By the turn of the 21st century, conservative churches that use contemporary Christian music in their service have become too numerous to count. In fact, it is difficult to find a church of any size that does not incorporate it in some way. These churches vary tremendously in terms of racial, ethnic, social, and economic make-up. Some churches that use contemporary music are more formal and structured, others retain a more casual character. Some are part of established denominations (from Catholic to Baptist to Methodist); others resist denominational structures and maintain their independence.

The central part played by contemporary worship music in these congregations draws on the Pietistic heritage discussed in chapter 1. In these churches the "worship time" (that is, the singing time) is often significantly longer than time spent for the sermon or communion, or any other aspect of the service. Many of the members say they are drawn to the church because of the worship experience created by the music. Like the Pietists in the colonial period, these conservative Christians are emphasizing experiential religion overrationalist religion; that is, religion one feels rather than religion one thinks about.

Top Christian Rock Musicians

Christian music is created by artists in just about every genre from rock to jazz to country to hip-hop. It is one of the fastest-growing segments of the music business and is now regularly charted by trade publications such as *Billboard* magazine. Here are some of the most prominent acts in Christian music.

Stephen Curtis Chapman, a five-time winner of the "Artist of the Year" Dove Award (given annually to honor Christian and gospel music)

dc Talk, the most successful of the many groups that blend hip-hop rhythms with Christian themes

Gospel Gangstaz, a rap group that has had many top-selling albums

Phil Joel, former singer for the Newsboys, has had two successful solo albums

Michael W. Smith, a favorite singer and songwriter, whose album "Worship Again" was a top seller in 2002

Rebecca St. James has had several top hits and won Dove Awards for her singing and songwriting

Third Day, a rock group that has won many Dove Awards

Singing her faith
Singer-songwriter Amy Grant is perhaps the most successful Christian "crossover" artist, blending Christian themes with popular music in a way that appeals to a mass audience.

But this music is important outside the church setting as well, as the music is available in Christian bookstores and is part of the day-to-day lives of believers. It is the cassettes and CDs for personal use at home and in the car that have made this industry as successful as it is. This is true both in terms of the financial success of the movement as well as the increased impact of the conservative Christian world on America.

GOD BLESS YOU
Sharing is
Caring
NEED KNOWS NO

Impact on American Social Issues

IT IS DIFFICULT TO DATE THE ORIGINS OF THE BROAD-BASED American commitment to social reform and volunteerism. Its seeds were certainly present with the earliest settlers in Massachusetts (shown in John Winthrop's 1630 sermon "A Model of Christian Charity"). But those seeds can be seen to have most fruitfully blossomed early in the 19th century when Protestant church leaders initiated numerous religious and social reform programs that collectively came to be known as the "Benevolent Kingdom."

While leaders on the frontier concentrated on evangelism (creating the movement known as the Second Great Awakening), leaders in the eastern cities created Christian literature, foreign missions, and temperance societies. They suggested that the Gospel provided the solution to all of society's problems. Christian concerns with slavery gave rise to calls for its abolition, and objections to the way women were treated led to the first attempts to change the status and role of women in the church and in society.

Abolition of Slavery

American religious opposition to the institution of slavery dates back to colonial days. Especially among the Quakers, antislavery societies appeared in several states in the late 1700s. Even among Methodists and Baptists antislavery views were widespread in both the North and the South during the revolutionary period. As regional divisions grew between North and South, abolitionists in the North led their denominations to exclude slaveholders from ministerial and missionary positions and even, in some cases, from church membership. The result was that the major denominations split into northern and southern bodies over slavery.

The revivals of the Second Great Awakening gave a boost to abolitionist sentiment, especially those led by Charles Grandison Finney. Abolitionists sought to end slavery completely. Theodore Dwight Weld (1803–1895) was perhaps the most notable example of this. Converted at one of Finney's revivals, Weld was not only convinced of the truth of the Gospel, but also found in it a calling to end slavery. He was later central to the founding of the American Antislavery Society in 1834. Weld arranged a series of debates at Lane Theological Seminary in Cincinnati, Ohio. The debates led some students to more fiercely oppose slavery; they then left Lane for Oberlin College, which was known for its commitment to abolition.

PRECEDING PAGE
Ring the bell
Salvation Army bell ringers are a familiar sight on American streets around Christmas. This Salvation Army employee is joined by then-Massachusetts Governor Jane Swift in 2001 to kick off that region's annual holiday appeal.

The Salvation Army Starts Marching

The Industrial Revolution in the late 19th century saw America's population move from rural farming communities to the cities and a rising tide of immigration from Europe. These factors created serious problems in the cities, such as overcrowding and poverty, that urban revivalists like Dwight L. Moody (1837–1899) sought to address through volunteerism and social reform flowing from their revivals.

Today many people think of the Salvation Army as a social service organization without necessarily realizing that it is also a church. The Salvation Army was founded by William and Catherine Booth in England in 1865. The church is in the Holiness tradition, but has an organizational structure based on a military model. Members are called soldiers, they wear uniforms, and achieve military-style ranks. As in many other Holiness churches, women can hold leadership positions. The Salvation Army came to America in 1880, where William and Catherine's daughter Evangeline became its most well-known spokesperson.

Initially focused on evangelism, and controversial for its unusual methods that included parading with brass bands, the Salvation Army soon learned that, for many people, poverty was a barrier to receiving the Gospel. William Booth wrote in *Darkest England and the Way Out* in 1890 that massive social service was a crucial aspect of evangelism.

The Salvation Army now has more than 1 million members in more than 100 countries. It provides homeless shelters, soup kitchens, and clothing to the needy. It also supports many programs designed to deal with the problems that create poverty. Treatment for drug and alcohol abuse, job training and counseling, even educational services are all central to the work of the Army.

Just Say No—to Alcohol

Many Christians in the 19th century came to think that poverty was, at least in part, rooted in the abuse of alcohol. While the fight for the 18th Amendment to the U.S. Constitution (banning the manufacture,

Carry A. Nation

Carry A. Nation was born in Kentucky, and, because she was not a strong child, she spent much of her time at home reading the Bible. At age 21 she married a young doctor who turned out to be an alcoholic. When their only daughter became seriously ill, she blamed it on her husband's drinking and left him.

After remarrying and moving to Texas, Nation dedicated herself to God and began lecturing against the evils of using tobacco and liquor. The family moved to Kansas, and there, Nation helped organize the Women's Christian Temperance Union (WCTU).

Partly because of the influence of the WCTU, in 1880 the voters of Kansas adopted a constitutional amendment prohibiting the manufacture and sale of intoxicating beverages, except for medicinal purposes. But Kansas saloonkeepers violated that law, and in 1900 Nation drew national attention by smashing up a saloon in Kiowa, Kansas. She was then asked by people from other counties to "save their towns from saloons." She promptly obliged, using stones and bricks wrapped in newspaper (later an iron rod strapped to her cane). Eventually, her tool of choice became an axe, and sales of pewter pins in the shape of an axe paid her numerous jail fines.

sale, and transportation of alcohol) could clearly be seen as a political effort, the political dimension was only one small part of this religious cause—one that has had a significant impact on American social values.

Conservative Christian opposition to the use of alcohol is so widespread in America that many people believe that it dates back to the nation's founders and especially the Puritans. But this is not the case. Puritans used wine in their church services and, although they opposed drunkenness they did not oppose moderate use of alcohol. However, by the 19th century, Christians, especially those in the Baptist and Methodist revivalist traditions, came to believe that the problems of the growing cities, especially poverty, were made much worse by the presence of alcohol. Thus the Temperance Movement was born.

The word "temperance" literally means moderation, but Temperance advocates worked to prohibit alcohol altogether. They worked first at the state level, and the first prohibition legislation was passed in Maine in 1846. The key advocate for the Maine prohibition law was Neal Dow (1804–1897), whose views on alcohol use were directly connected to his understanding of Christianity. Between 1906 and 1917, 26 states enacted prohibition legislation.

By the end of the 19th century, efforts to prohibit alcohol were focused on the national level. The Anti Saloon League was founded in 1893 and Methodist minister Alpha J. Kynett (1829–?) led the organization to become one of the two main organizations in favor of the 18th Amendment—the other being the Women's Christian Temperance Union (WCTU). The 18th Amendment was passed by Congress in 1914 and was ratified by two-thirds of the states in 1919.

Much of the movement's efforts focused on convincing Christians of the evils of alcohol. Temperance advocates encouraged ministers to preach on this topic and they organized Christians, young and old, to take temperance pledges. One of the more colorful characters of the time was Carry Nation (1846–1911), who traveled about Kansas with her Bible and her hatchet, destroying saloons and preaching about the evils of alcohol (see page 67).

Another of the more interesting ways that temperance advocates worked to change public perceptions of alcohol was in popular culture. For the first time, relatively inexpensive printing processes were available and temperance novels were widely distributed. These novels told relatively predictable, moralistic stories, in which alcohol

On the river for life
Evangelical missionary John Mortimer pilots a boat on a river in the Amazon jungle of northeast Peru as he takes his family and local people to church meeting.

is clearly seen to bring about the downfall of the main character in the story.

Although the 18th Amendment was repealed in 1933, the efforts of the Temperance Movement to shape American attitudes, particularly American Christian attitudes, concerning the use of alcohol had a lasting impact on American society.

Missions

Christian commitment to missionary work has shaped church life and social values in America, as well as ideas about America's place in the world and its responsibilities to other nations.

Christians have funded missions to evangelize Native Americans, slaves, and former slaves. They have funded urban missions to feed, house, and clothe the poor. But it has been foreign missions that have most attracted the attention of American church members. In 1900, there were more than 5,000 American missionaries around the world; by 1936, that number had grown to 13,000. Numerous missionary societies were founded to recruit and fund missionaries and to help missionary efforts administratively. These included the Woman's Union Missionary Society (1861); the Student Volunteer Movement for Foreign Missions (1886); the Missionary Education Movement (1902); and the Laymen's Missionary Movement (1907). In 1917 several societies banded together to found an interdenominational association to oversee mission societies, called the Foreign Missions Association.

Missionaries returned to the U.S. periodically to visit churches and raise funds and they brought with them vivid stories of exotic places in Africa, China, and India. American Christian children grew up admiring missionaries like Hudson Taylor (1832–1905) and David Livingstone (1813–1873) and many dreamed of becoming missionaries.

In the middle of the 20th century mission societies were troubled by the same divisions occurring in Protestantism itself. Fundamentalist factions continued to believe conversion to fundamental Christianity was the only route to salvation. Modernists, however, began to struggle with issues related to cultural imperialism. They were concerned about how much of what they understood of the Gospel was based on their own culture and how much was tied to an eternal truth. They wondered whether it was right to impose their own culture on others.

By the end of the 20th century even the more Fundamentalist missionaries had come to value the idea of making the Gospel fit better into existing local cultures. They tried to sort out what they thought were the essentials of the Gospel and separate those from its cultural packaging. This method served to present the Gospel message in different ways to different cultures.

Fundamentalist Views on the Role of Women

Fundamentalists have been very outspoken regarding the role of women. However, gender relationships in American Fundamentalism are much more flexible than many people realize. While most people ascribe traditional family values to Fundamentalism, the definition of traditional family values is more complicated than one might think. And, in addition to traditional family values there is also a well-developed strain of Fundamentalism committed to equality between the sexes.

What contemporary Fundamentalists mean by the traditional

family is an idealized version of the late Victorian middle class family, which includes a sharp division between the roles of men and women. This notion of the traditional family is a product of the Industrial Revolution of the late 1800s, during which people moved from the country to the cities and there developed a distinct middle class. This new middle class could afford the division of labor idealized in traditional family values: The father is off in the rough and tumble business world, and the mother is at home creating a refuge for the father at the end of the day, and nurturing children through a privileged childhood.

Late 20th century legal and cultural reforms concerning women and women's rights challenged these sorts of families and led Fundamentalists to seek a return to those ideals; much of their political agenda still revolves around these family issues—feminism, abortion, gay rights, education, and even taxation.

Since the 1970s there has also been an active, well-developed movement within Fundamentalism to secure equality for men and women. While some in this movement rejected the label feminist, many of those who promote these views do identify themselves as feminists. Calling themselves Christian Feminists, Biblical Feminists, or Evangelical Feminists, they call for women's equality in marriage, women's ordination, complete equality in all Christian ministry and the use of gender inclusive language in liturgy, songs, theology, and even biblical translation (using a phrase such as "people and God" instead of "man and God," for example). They believe that, properly interpreted, the Bible commands gender equality.

The Question of Husband and Wives

An illustration of the way Fundamentalists understand the Bible will make this more clear. Those Fundamentalists who argue that women should not be pastors and that wives are to be subordinate to their husbands point to certain passages in the New Testament that the Biblical Feminists believe they misinterpret.

A common discussion is over the notion of "headship," since the traditionalists argue that the Bible is clear in making husbands "heads" over their wives. Biblical Feminists ask what the apostle Paul meant when he argued that the man was the "head" of the woman (Ephesians 5:23). They then go to the original version of the text, which Paul wrote in Greek, and argue that the Greek word *kephale*, which is translated as

WOMEN AND EARLY FUNDAMENTALISTS

Among the earliest activists for women's rights, especially for the right to vote, were Evangelical Christians. They believed that women were the more nurturing gender and that, because of this, their influence on society was desperately needed. In fact, it seems that antifeminism did not become the dominant perspective in Protestant Fundamentalism until well into the 1920s.

There is evidence of early Fundamentalist support for women as pastors, women's public preaching, and women's active involvement in ministry leadership. When Fundamentalists needed greater efforts for aggressive evangelization, women were encouraged to take leadership roles.

But by the late 1940s and 1950s the larger culture was urging women back into the home and Fundamentalism followed suit, limiting leadership roles for women. This move toward limiting women's roles was not a Fundamentalist reaction in opposition to the larger culture, but a development in accordance with, and part of, that larger culture.

"head," does not include the idea of "authority over," as it does in English. Had Paul wanted to denote "authority over" he would have used a different term. They say *kephale* means head as in "source" (the head of a river, for example), and argue that Paul is referring to the creation account in which Adam was created first and Eve was made from his rib. They then cite Paul's later statement that although woman originally came from man, through the birthing process all men come from women. They conclude that taking these passages in light of Paul's statement in Galatians that there "is no male or female in Christ" (Galatians 3:28) the Bible necessarily teaches equality between men and women.

The proper relationship between husbands and wives, for the Biblical Feminists, is "mutual submission." They point out that the passage in Ephesians (5:22) that commands wives to submit to their husbands is immediately preceded by a command that all Christians submit to one another. Biblical Feminists argue that Paul's command that husbands love their wives includes an assumption that wives should also love their husbands.

On the issue of women in leadership roles in religious institutions, Biblical Feminists argue that Paul may indeed have commanded women to be silent in church (Ephesians 14:34), but he seems to undermine an interpretation that would apply this to all Christians in all contexts when, a few short verses later he describes the proper manner in which women should prophesy (with their heads covered, Ephesians 14:34). Biblical Feminists prefer the King James translation of 1 Corinthians 13:12, in which Paul says he does not permit women to take away authority from men. That does not mean, in their view, that women cannot have authority, but merely that they are not to take authority that is not rightly theirs.

The point here is not to evaluate the interpretation of each group, but rather, to observe that within this conservative Christian world there really is more than one way to read these Bible verses.

Promise Keepers

In addition to conflicts over appropriate roles for women, conservative Christianity has also fed a growing men's movement in America. The Promise Keepers, a men's organization founded in 1990, has traditional views on the roles of men and women and the relationship be-

A promise kept
Hundreds of thousands of members of the Promise Keepers organization filled the Mall in Washington, D.C., in front of the U.S. Capitol Building at this 1997 rally.

tween them. However, it presents these views in softer terms than others who harshly demand women's submission to men. There are has been much debate over what values traditional Promise Keepers really respect.

Promise Keepers brings men together in revival services and calls on them to repent for putting their careers first while neglecting the needs of their wives and children, to mend their relationships with other men, especially with their fathers, and to work for racial reconciliation. Early on, Promise Keepers received much public attention due to the media interest in its massive gatherings held at sports facilities. Those huge, public campaigns led to the development of small, local groups made up of men who had attended the rallies and who kept meeting together regularly.

The organization experienced rapid growth in the 1990s. In 1996 Promise Keepers' rallies around the country drew crowds of more than 1 million men and the national organization itself had a budget of more than $100 million. But before too long Promise Keepers encountered management and financial difficulties that ultimately weakened its national influence, though the smaller local groups have continued to thrive.

The Black Church and the Civil Rights Movement

The most important and successful social revolution brought about by religion was the Civil Rights Movement that began in the African-American churches in the 1950s and continues today.

A lasting imprint
The actions of Rosa Parks in 1955 (shown here being fingerprinted in early 1956) energized the nascent Civil Rights Movement, a movement largely led by African-American Christian church leaders in the South.

The Civil War brought an end to slavery but there remained tremendous injustice and racism in both the North and the South. The Civil Rights Movement focused primarily on addressing structural racism in the forms of discrimination in the North and segregation and restrictions on voting rights in the South. The laws that mandated white/black segregation in the South are often called Jim Crow laws—named for a fictional black character imitated by white entertainers. Under Jim Crow, blacks and whites had segregated schools, drinking fountains, restrooms, public swimming pools, seats on buses, and entrances to movie theatres. Almost every public activity was racially segregated.

In addition to the consistently inferior facilities for blacks and the humiliation of submitting to Jim Crow laws, African Americans who tried to assert their basic rights also faced the serious threat of physical violence, including lynchings and church bombings.

The Civil Rights Movement is often said to have begun with the bus boycott in Montgomery, Alabama, in 1955. The Montgomery public bus system was segregated, as were most public facilities at the time. Rosa Parks (b. 1913), an African-American woman and Methodist activist, sparked the boycott that eventually led to the desegregation of the bus system, when she refused to give up her bus seat to a white man. Parks was arrested, and local leaders called a meeting at the Dexter Avenue Baptist Church, pastored by Rev. Dr. Martin Luther King, Jr. (1929–1968). Just about every black person in Montgomery agreed not to ride the buses until the law was changed. Blacks walked miles to work and organized car pools to help one another.

The boycott was declared illegal and many Black Church leaders were arrested for violating that law. Within a year, though, the bus system was desegregated. With the support of African-American church leaders, schools in Alabama, Arkansas, and Mississippi were desegregated; lunch counters in North Carolina, Mississippi, Virginia, and Tennessee were desegregated; and African-American voters were registered all over the South. It was, and continues to be, a powerful example of faith influencing society in positive and lasting ways.

5

The Impact of Evangelicals on American Politics

AS WE HAVE DISCUSSED, THE EVANGELICAL TRADITIONS (ESPECIALLY the Baptists) were in many ways centrally responsible for the First Amendment clause guaranteeing the separation of church and state. In some ways, however, this idea has come full circle, as many evangelical Christians have a very different view of the appropriate relationship between religion and politics. This chapter will explore how their views have changed, the cultural forces that brought about those changes, and the role Baptists, Methodists, and other Evangelicals now play in American politics as what has been called the religious right or the New Christian Right.

After the Scopes Monkey Trial (see page 39), Fundamentalists realized that their views, at odds with secular society and science, would not be the dominant version of Protestantism in America. They responded to this realization by turning inward and building institutions that would enable them to maintain their faith within their own cultural system and to pass that along to their children. These institutions included churches and Bible colleges to train their own pastors. They created religious organizations to produce Sunday school materials, send out missionaries, and explore evangelistic uses of new technology. From the 1920s through the 1950s, Fundamentalists were relatively content to live within their own world. Their beliefs about the end times made it easy for them to consider the rest of the culture a lost cause. They simply wanted to protect their faith, raise their children in it, and save as many souls as they could.

If the division between Fundamentalists and Modernists at the turn of the century had been largely a theological one (see page 37), by the middle of the 20th century the Fundamentalists faced another version of this conflict. The social upheaval of the 1960s and 1970s was seen by Fundamentalists seriously limiting their ability to continue to maintain their culture.

When the New Christian Right became suddenly public in the 1980 elections, thanks to the influence of conservative Christian organizations in the election of President Ronald Reagan, observers scrambled to make sense of the movement. Many were surprised at this groundswell of conservative religion in politics and asked, "How is it that no one saw this coming?" Many had thought American Fundamentalism was dead, or at least that it was in the process of dying out.

PRECEDING PAGE
Seeking votes
Televangelist Pat Robertson ran for the Republican presidential nomination in 1988. Although Robertson lost, the attention his campaign received was another sign of the growing power of conservative Christians in national politics.

But religious conservatives around the country were growing increasingly unhappy over the restrictions placed on religious influence in public life. Many of these changes—such as the increasing availability of legal abortion, the gender and sexual revolutions, what they perceived as the influence of communism, and the increasing willingness of the government to intrude in the running of their churches and private Christian schools—came as a result of a wider interpretation of the section in the First Amendment that prohibits the establishment of a state religion. While these troubling cultural changes were taking place, there were also important developments within the conservative Christian world. Specifically, the end times theology that had led Fundamentalists to withdraw from the world was replaced by a much more world-engaging perspective.

America as a Christian Nation

There was another development within this conservative Christian world that was important in politicizing religion in this period. This was the growing popularity of the idea that America was a Christian nation with a special calling from God to be a saving light to the world. Numerous conservative Christian writers produced books, study manuals, and collections of primary materials they believed documented the Christian origins of America. The evidence they point to ranges from the diaries of Christopher Columbus as he set sail for the New World and Puritan sermons emphasizing the covenant settlers had made with God, to the many statements of the nation's founders about the central importance of religion for a free society. These Christians identified America as God's chosen nation, destined to be the earthly version of the Kingdom of God. As they saw it, in recent history America had slipped from its moorings and had lost its way. The remedy was to be found as good Christians once again involved themselves in the decisions of the society, working to restore the nation's mission.

These materials were used by ministers, Bible study leaders, Sunday school teachers and Christian educators to reshape the conservative Christian sense of who they were and how they were to be part of this society. Wednesday night Bible study classes were replaced by courses in Christian American history. Church members made use of workbooks and study manuals as they explored this topic. Such study sessions were often followed by tactical sessions teaching church members how to become involved in politics. Churches held workshops and training sessions on how the political process works, how to write letters to newspapers and elected officials, how to become involved in political parties, how to work on political campaigns, and even how to run for political office.

Making an Impact in Schools

At the same time, conservative Christian attitudes about what God expected of them in terms of participation in civil society were changing. These new attitudes pushed them toward political involvement. Changes in the larger culture increasingly generated concern that served to pull them into politics, as well. Many of those changes occurred with regard to education.

Through the 1800s, Protestants saw public schools as religiously neutral American institutions, promoting a commitment to democracy, freedom, equality, and religious tolerance. This view was not unchallenged, as many Catholics saw the American public schools system as religiously biased against their tradition and established separate Catholic schools for their children. Protestants, at the time, saw such late 19th-century Catholic efforts as divisive and anti-patriotic. In fact, public schools have been called the "established church" in America because it has often been in the context of public school that

What Is Right and What Is Left?

The terms *right* and *left* have come to define the two major philosophies of government and politics in America. They are very broad terms and their definitions would probably be disputed by people on both sides. It might best be thought of as a wide scale with many degrees of difference. With that in mind, here are very general ways to think of the two sides.

Right

Conservative in outlook, most often Republican. Believes in conventional family values, in keeping government out of people's lives as much as possible. In general prefers to keep things as they are in economics and social policy. Would rather see more power given to states and local communities. Perceived as being more oriented toward big businesses.

Left

Liberal in outlook, most often Democratic. More ready to use government programs to create solutions to social problems. Generally more focused on using market forces to spur social change. More willing to force change onto institutions and markets. Perceived as being more oriented toward consumers.

Americans have shaped the moral basis for the culture and constructed a shared national identity for its people.

However, by the late 1960s, the perception of more conservative Protestants began to change as the public schools took on an increasingly secular character. This process was largely driven by a series of Supreme Court decisions about the acceptable level of religious activity in public schools.

The Courts Make the Case

To understand these cases and these issues, we should first touch on a couple of points about the U.S. Constitution and the legal relationship between church and state. The First Amendment says, "Congress shall make no law respecting an establishment of religion or prohibiting the free exercise thereof." An "establishment of religion" in this sense is one that is formally supported by the government. And it is important to note that these prohibitions were first addressed only to the federal government (Congress). In fact, when the Bill of Rights was ratified several states did have state-supported churches.

During the period following the Civil War, the 14th Amendment was ratified making it unconstitutional for any state to deprive a U.S. citizen of his or her rights without due process. By the 1940s the Supreme Court ruled, in *Cantwell v. Connecticut*, that freedom of religion was among those rights and that states could not establish churches or prohibit the free exercise of religion. In theory this seems straightforward enough, but in practice it actually become quite complicated. For example, the courts have said it is inappropriate for the government to tax churches, but churches receive government services anyway. For example, they get fire and police services at the expense of those who do pay taxes. As a result, there are still many Supreme Court cases seeking to sort out the relationship between the government and religious institutions.

Perhaps the most controversial of these court cases, and one most relevant here, was the first of the school prayer decisions in 1962, *Engel v. Vitale*. The New York Board of Regents, which oversaw the state's public schools, wrote a prayer to be said by school children at the beginning of each school day. Specifically designed to be acceptable to a variety of religions, the prayer, nonetheless, was not acceptable to some of parents and their children, so they sued. They claimed that the prayer written and sponsored by the state was a violation of the First Amendment clause known as the Establishment Clause. The Supreme Court agreed.

In a second controversial case a year later, *Abington Township School District v. Shemmp*, the Court repeated its prohibition of state-sponsored school prayer, and ruled on appropriate and inappropriate uses of the Bible in public school classrooms. The law at issue required public school children to begin their day with the Lord's Prayer (a specifically Christian prayer) and/or the reading of a chapter of the Bible. The Court ruled that this form of Bible reading was devotional, that is, part of a specific religion, and therefore in violation of the First Amendment's Establishment Clause.

However, in the same ruling, the Supreme Court also said that teaching about religion and using the Bible in public school classrooms to do so was not only permissible but necessary. It said that educated persons ought to know about religion and its importance in history, art, and literature.

A Key Decision

Here is the prayer that the New York State Board of Regents wrote for students to say:

"Almighty God, we acknowledge our dependence upon Thee, and we beg They blessings upon us, our parents, our teachers and our Country."

Here is some of what the U.S. Supreme Court said in its 1962 decision to remove the prayer from school classrooms:

> *The Petitioners [parents opposing the use of the prayer] contend among other things that the state laws requiring or permitting use of the Regent's prayer must be struck down as a violation of the Establishment Clause because that prayer was composed by governmental officials as part of a government program to further religious beliefs. For this reason, the petitioners argue, the State's use of the prayer in its public school system breaches the constitutional wall of separation between Church and State. We agree with that contention since we think that the constitutional prohibition against laws respecting an establishment of religion must at least mean that in this country it is no part of the business of the government to compose official prayers for any group of the American people to recite as part of a religious program carried on by government. ...There can be no doubt that New York's state prayer program officially establishes the religious beliefs embodied in the Regents' prayer.*

Doing their own thing
In response to prayer being "taken out" of public schools by various court rulings, some churches started their own elementary schools, such as this one in West Virginia in 1975.

These two decisions were troubling to conservative Christian parents, who saw them as an attempt to remove God from public schools. While these decisions really only addressed state-sponsored prayer and devotional Bible reading, to conservative Christians, it seemed the decisions banned prayer, the Bible, and God from public schools.

Teaching Values in School

Another area of major conflict between the conservative Christians on the religious right and the larger American culture is the teaching of sex education and moral values. In fact many conservative Christians abandoned public schools over this issue. While polls indicate that most Americans (conservative Christians included) believe that public schools should teach human biological reproduction, the disagreement comes over issues of values, especially as those values relate to sex education.

Conservative Christian parents were deeply offended by public school classes that taught that values were subjective, meaning that each person had to arrive at his or her own values. This directly contradicts their view that values are absolute and given by God for humans to obey. So classes that did not argue that abstinence (not having sex) was the only option for unmarried young people, or that taught that abortion was a matter of a woman's right to choose, or that same-sex relationships were acceptable options, were deeply offensive to these Christians.

The Battle Over Creation

After the Scopes Monkey Trial, Fundamentalists did not give up on efforts to fight for teaching creationism in public schools, but by the 1970s it was becoming increasingly clear that they would not succeed. It is important to understand that creationism is more than just a story about the origins of life, as described in the book of Genesis. To Christians, creationism considers not only how we got here, but why we are here.

These Christians take literally the book of Genesis, which writes that God created the heavens and the earth in six days. Beginning in the 1970s, there developed a widely held version of creationism called Creation Science. Henry Morris (b.1917), of the Institute for Creation Research, was one of the most well-known promoters of this view. Creation scientists argue that modern scientific methods can prove the biblical account of creation to be correct. They developed arguments out of the fossil records in support of their theories, which are widely taught in Christian private schools and home schools.

Religious right activists continue in their efforts to promote the teaching of creation in public schools. Today, they most often argue that both "theories" (evolution and creation) should be presented in the interest of open inquiry. During the 1980s legislation was introduced in 26 states to require creationism to be taught alongside evolution. Arkansas and Louisiana were the only two states to pass such bills, and eventually the courts ruled those laws unconstitutional.

In 1999, the Kansas School Board received nationwide attention when it tried a different approach. Kansas has a competency exam that prospective high school students must pass. For a time, the school board removed evolution from the exam, giving local school boards the option to stop teaching it. The school board member who was a major force behind this effort was defeated in the next election and evolution was put back on the test, but the case demonstrates that, even after nearly a century of conflict, this issue is not resolved.

As conservative Christian parents saw these changes taking place in public education they became increasingly uncomfortable with having their children in public schools. This led to three responses. First, many became involved in politics in an effort to roll back the tide of change. They worked at the national level in congressional and even presidential campaigns, and they worked at the local level on school boards and city councils. Issues related to public education were the key that led to the rise of the religious right, which we will explore shortly.

Some of the religious conservatives came to believe that efforts to reform public schools would ultimately fail and chose to remove their children from them. Many religious conservatives established private Christian schools. As a third response, others began teaching their children at home. These last two responses also pushed conservative Christian parents to become involved in politics as they faced repeated efforts on the part of state governments to regulate their private schools and home schools.

ERA

Here is the entire text of the proposed Equal Rights Amendment to the Constitution:

Section 1. Equality of rights under the law shall not be denied or abridged by the United States or by any state on account of sex.

Section 2. The Congress shall have the power to enforce, by appropriate legislation, the provisions of this article.

Section 3. This amendment shall take effect two years after the date of ratification.

Family, Gender, and the ERA

In addition to education, issues concerning gender and family played an important role in making conservative Christians more politically active. On March 22, 1972, Congress passed the Equal Rights Amendment (ERA) and sent it to the states for ratification. The Amendment guaranteed equal protection for women under the law. Within a year, 22 states had ratified it; however, by the end of the seven-year time limit only 35 states had ratified it instead of the needed 38. The deadline was extended, but no more ratifications were forthcoming. And, although the ERA has been repeatedly introduced in Congress, it has not been passed again.

The efforts of the religious right are often credited with the defeat of the Equal Rights Amendment. Religious conservatives feared that legally mandated equal treatment of men and women would result in legally mandated identical treatment, which they opposed. Religious conservatives believe that God created men and women to be different and that legal structures need to recognize those differences. In addition to this point, ERA opponents argued that the Constitution already requires legal equality for women and that the proposed amendment provided no significant benefits but did pose significant risks.

In opposition to the amendment, the national Christian organization called Eagle Forum/STOP the ERA, led by Phyllis Schlafly, organized local chapters nationwide. They led the opposition, arguing that the amendment would eliminate legal protections for women, place women in military combat, legalize gay and lesbian marriages, guarantee continued legal status for abortion rights, and mandate unisex bathrooms. With the 1980 elections, which resulted in the election of Republican president Ronald Reagan and major successes by religious right candidates, anti-ERA forces had gained more strength and the hopes of feminist activists were dimmed.

The Issue of Abortion

In January of 1973 the U.S. Supreme Court issued a controversial opinion that both appalled and energized conservative religious people. *Roe v. Wade* brought a hodge-podge of different state laws and regulations regarding abortion into one national standard. Dividing pregnancy into three trimesters, the Court prohibited limitations on a woman's right to have an abortion in the first three months of pregnancy—the first trimester. The Court allowed for more regulation in the second and third trimesters, because it saw increased risks for mother and fetus. However, even in the third trimester, states cannot regulate abortion when it is necessary to protect the life or health of the mother. Health, in this case, has been defined by the courts in very broad terms.

Conservative Christians have understood this decision as legalizing abortion on demand during the entire nine months of pregnancy and have fought vigorously, in the courts, the legislatures, and in the forum of public opinion, to change that. The issue has served as a central focus for building the religious right.

Initial efforts of the Right to Life movement, which is what anti-abortion groups call themselves (the opposing forces call themselves Pro-Choice), included basic electoral politics, letter writing, providing services to women facing crisis pregnancies, and so on. During the late 1970s and through the 1980s, conservative churches organized for political involvement, with the abortion issue as a catalyst. Frequently, the pastor at a church would agree to the showing of a Right to Life film in place of the usual mid-week service. After viewing videos with titles such as *Assignment Life, Eclipse of Reason*, and *Whatever Happened to the Human Race?*, church members were encouraged (often by the pastor himself from the pulpit) to become involved in a Right to Life ministry. Involvement might include volunteering time and/or

Concerned Women for America

In 1979, Beverley LaHaye started the antifeminist organization Concerned Women for America (CWA). Beverley is married to Tim LaHaye, religious right leader and best-selling author of the *Left Behind* series (see page 53). The purpose of CWA is to provide an alternative forum for women who do not feel well represented by the feminist movement. Initially focused on opposing the Equal Rights Amendment but now with a broader agenda, the group is organized around women's Bible study groups. This makes this group decidedly local and grassroots in its orientation. Informed observers speculate that it may have as many as 500,000 members.

In 1985, LaHaye sought to make her organization more national in scope and she moved it to Washington, D.C. Even there, though, CWA took a different approach from the other religious right groups by operating a legal affairs division that takes legal cases that have precedent-setting possibilities on issues of central concern to CWA. The cases this organization tackles have to do with church and state concerns, such as those affecting the content of textbooks.

money to a crisis pregnancy center, lobbying on legislation and/or court appointments, working in political campaigns, or participating in demonstrations.

Church members frequently moved from involvement on the abortion issue to work on other issues on the Christian right's agenda, but their initial introduction to political activity was often on the abortion issue.

Right-to-Life organizations fought to change abortion laws on several fronts. They had much hope during the Reagan administrations that justices who did not support legalized abortion would be appointed to the Supreme Court and might eventually overturn the 5 to 4 *Roe v. Wade* decision. Efforts were made in Congress to go around the Supreme Court by saying that the Court did not have jurisdiction on the issue. The groups worked with sympathetic members of Congress to propose a host of bills that would limit abortions in one way or another. For the most part these efforts were not successful and Right-to-Lifers became increasingly frustrated.

By the mid-1980s a new tactic became increasingly common: civil disobedience. Operation Rescue was founded by Randall Terry (b.1959) in Binghamton, New York, but Right-to-Lifers around the country adopted his strategies. "Rescuers" would meet at secret locations early Saturday morning and go to an abortion clinic, where they would sit in front of the doors carrying signs and praying, thus trying to prevent doctors, staff, and patients from entering. This, they argued, precluded any abortions from taking place on that day, and therefore saved lives. Trained in nonviolent civil disobedience tactics developed during the Civil Rights Movement, rescuers passively resisted arrest and thereby kept the doors closed as long as possible. Many Christian right leaders and lay people spent time in jail or paid fines for trespassing during the 1980s.

By the 1990s, though, the movement began to dwindle, especially in the face of strong confrontation with the legal system. The federal government used anti-racketeering legislation (legislation that established huge fines for anyone illegally impeding the functioning of a legal business, laws originally designed to fight organized crime) to levy huge fines on the protesters and their organizations. The result of this was that many religious right activists moved on to other issues, as we shall see. Some, however, moved on to violent forms of protest that included the murder of abortion doctors and the bombing of abortion clinics.

Gay and Lesbian Rights

The abortion issue has been the cornerstone of the Christian right's support of what they perceive as the traditional family. While questions about the point at which humans become persons with legal rights and a claim to life have dominated the debate, in many ways the status of the family, as Fundamentalists understand it, is really what is at issue in the abortion debate.

By the early 1990s a significant shift took place in the strategy of the Christian right, moving from the abortion issue to opposition to gay rights. It is not that the Christian right no longer cared about abortion, or that they had not always opposed gay rights, only that there was a shift in emphasis, which was especially apparent in the efforts to get fellow Christians involved in politics.

The gay rights issue lent itself well to the Christian right's political strategies. It can, like the abortion issue, be framed as central to the survival of the traditional family. Particularly threatening to conservative Christian parents are efforts to teach about homosexuality in schools in a way that contradicted teachings the children would receive at home. Similar to the topic of abortion, gay rights can also be used as an issue that motivates people to become involved in politics in ways that more complicated, less divisive issues cannot.

The issue of gay rights lends itself to compromise and piecemeal efforts—especially local efforts—in a way that the abortion issue never did. Abortion, for conservative Christians, was all or nothing. Once they framed the issue as protecting human life from the moment of conception, Right-to-Lifers could accept nothing short of a complete ban on all abortions. They could not generate broad-based public support for this extreme position. Political success was also difficult to achieve because the Supreme Court's protection of abortion rights, at a constitutional level, largely limited the potential battles to the appointment of Supreme Court Justices, proposed constitutional amendments, and a few other issues.

Many of the battles over gay rights, on the other hand, are fought in state legislatures and on local school boards. This has two advantages for the Christian right. First, the Christian right is most organized

Words and Pictures to Support Their Cause

A number of groups used the power of words and pictures to help increase support against expanding the rights of gays and lesbians in America.

In the fall 1992, Oregon and Colorado had anti-gay initiatives on their statewide ballots. A video called *The Gay Agenda*, made in support of those laws, was used extensively in the campaign against revising the rules regarding gays in the military. That issue had come up early in the administration of President Bill Clinton, elected in 1992. The video was distributed widely on Capitol Hill and at the Pentagon.

In the first half of 1993, almost every major group associated with the Christian right has produced a package of anti-gay rights material to be sent to their supporters. The Rutherford Institute, which once focused on legal defense of abortion opponents and Christian schools, sent a package arguing that proposed gay rights bills in a number of states would violate the religious freedom of Christians.

James Kennedy's Coral Ridge Ministries in Florida sent out a national petition to keep gays out of the military. In October 1993, Concerned Women of America sent a fundraising appeal in the form of a survey. The "Homosexual Agenda Survey" was accompanied by a letter alleging that, among other things, "sex kits" were being passed out to children in schools.

and effective at the local level. Many who share these traditional family values have been elected to school boards and city councils, for example. Second, the Christian right will undoubtedly lose some of these smaller battles but will win others.

The Religious Right Moves to Washington

By the late 1970s, religious conservatives were growing increasingly concerned about the cultural changes they saw around them, and conservative churches began to explore new perspectives that led to more active political involvement. A handful of conservative political leaders in Washington started building a grassroots network to bring about change. Initially there were four groups that made up the organized political groups of the Christian right: the National Christian Action Coalition (NCAC), the Religious Roundtable, the Christian Voice, and the Moral Majority.

In 1978 Bob Billings founded NCAC in response to attempts by the Internal Revenue Service to use tax exempt status as a tool to foster racial desegregation in private schools. Shortly thereafter, with the help of Christian right leaders Richard Viguerie and Paul Weyrich, Ed McAteer founded the Religious Roundtable to encourage Fundamentalist pastors to become involved in politics and to teach them how to do so. Christian Voice was founded by Pastors Robert Grant and Richard

Zone to oppose a gay rights measure in California. It was later run by Gary Jarmin. This organization became well known when it issued its "moral approval rating," ranking Congress members on various issues of concern to conservative Christians.

In 1979, Jerry Falwell founded the Moral Majority, which was to become the most controversial and well known of these early groups. In fact, this group became so well known that its name became for many a way to refer to the entire conservative Christian political movement. Falwell's argument was that the vast majority of Americans agreed with him and that the problem was that political leaders in Washington were out of touch with real America. As he saw it, it the "moral majority" of Americans could be energized to take a stand against the liberalism they already opposed and that the drift away from godliness could be stopped.

Falwell, pastor of the Thomas Road Baptist Church in Lynchburg, Virginia, was already successful as a television preacher with a national audience. At first his presence on the political scene received much attention. He was the story the media loved to tell during the 1980 presidential election, although most observers now believe that he was given more attention than was probably warranted. Although Falwell had a national television audience for his *Old Time Gospel Hour*, the Moral Majority itself consisted mainly of a mailing list of subscribers. To some extent it seems that the amount of attention given the Moral Majority had as much to do with the way American politics works as it does with the amount of political clout the organization actually had. The media wanted a good story and liberal opponents of the Moral Majority raised lots of money by convincing people the organization was a real threat. Equally important, the conservative supporters of the religious right raised lots of money convincing people that the Moral Majority was their power center in Washington, a power center they had lacked for a very long time.

Falwell's ability to attract attention served the new political movement well, and he was a major voice through the first half of the 1980s. By 1986, however, Falwell suddenly announced that he was disbanding the Moral Majority because the confrontational style of the organization had served its purpose. He was replacing it with the Liberty Federation. However, the new organization never amounted to much and Falwell returned to pastoring his church and building Liberty

University, making only occasional comments about specific political conflicts and issues. He spoke out in favor of the civil disobedience of Operation Rescue and against the execution of a born-again woman on death row in Texas. For the most part, though, he left the political organizing to his successors.

Focus on the Family

There are several groups in the conservative religious coalition that have important political dimensions, but claim not to be political. While these groups do not organize voters or lobby elected officials,

Leader of the Moral Majority

Reverend Jerry Falwell (b.1933) is a graduate of Baptist Bible College in Springfield, Missouri, and has been pastor of Thomas Road Baptist Church in Lynchburg, Virginia, since it was founded in 1956. He is also chancellor of Liberty University there, which he started in 1971. The church currently has about 22,000 members and the school has 14,000 students.

Falwell appears regularly on the Christian television show *Old Time Gospel Hour*, which is seen on 225 stations. He founded and led the Moral Majority and its successor, the Liberty Federation, and founded the Elim Home for Alcoholics and Liberty Godparent Home for Unwed Mothers.

Falwell jumped into the political arena in the 1980s through his leadership in the Moral Majority. He tried to influence the government to support legislation to ban abortion, among other conservative issues.

Controversy has always followed Falwell, from conservative Christians who claimed his deep involvement in politics was unseemly, to his connection to the PTL Network scandal in 1987. The PTL had been run by Reverend Jim Bakker, who was forced to resign when he was discovered to be sleeping with a prostitute. An investigation also revealed misappropriation of funds. In the midst of the scandal, Falwell assumed leadership of the PTL and praised Bakker's ministry.

Most recently, Falwell stirred up controversy again when he stated publicly that the terrorist attacks on America on September 11, 2001, were punishment from God for the nation's liberal attitudes toward homosexuality.

it is worthwhile to examine their claim to be outside politics. Focus on the Family is an example of one such group. Founder James Dobson (b. 1936) first received national attention for his 1989 radio interview with convicted murderer Theodore Bundy. Dobson's daily radio show includes advice on marriage and parenting as well as what he calls Christian psychology, and airs on more than 15,000 stations nationwide.

Focus on the Family does have a Washington-based political arm called the Family Research Council. But the larger organization itself is politically active in that it shapes listeners' views on issues that have deep political implications, such as gay and lesbian rights, women's rights, and educational issues.

Pat Robertson and the Christian Coalition

It would be hard to overestimate the importance of televangelism to the religious right. In many ways televangelism gave birth to the movement; then, in its next phase, it gave it its distinct character. While the Moral Majority was receiving the media attention, Pat Robertson (b.1930) was organizing his *700 Club* audience into a "non-profit educational foundation" he called the Freedom Forum. The Moral Majority may have been essentially a Washington-based mailing list, but the Freedom Forum was a grassroots, church-based network promoting Christian interest in politics.

Like the Moral Majority, though, the Freedom Forum was suddenly disbanded. This happened when Robertson announced in 1986 that he would seek the Republican nomination for president. The Freedom Forum was replaced by the Christian Coalition, an organization that would become the leading religious right group during the 1990s.

Robertson's candidacy was not taken very seriously, initially. But in the Michigan primary on August 5, 1988, it looked for a time, and especially to his supporters, as though Robertson had a real shot at the nomination. Robertson beat both George H. Bush and popular conservative congressman Jack Kemp.

The presidential nomination process is complicated and the rules vary from state to state. Rather than having an early primary election in which only party members vote (as most states do), Michigan follows the convention system. In this system, candidates recruit delegates to go to nominating meetings and support them. The grassroots or-

Mover and shaker
Ralph Reed led the Christian Coalition into national prominence in the 1980s. The group of conservative Christians used their voice to express opinions on a wide variety of issues and to support candidates that agreed with their views.

ganizing of Freedom Forum/Christian Coalition was exactly what was needed to win nominating conventions.

Robertson's Pentecostal religious views, and his belief in political conspiracy views (later published in 1991 in his book *The New World Order*), proved to be serious liabilities during the campaign. He was criticized for saying that God had called him to run for office, for believing that prayer had saved the Christian Broadcasting Network's radio towers from a hurricane, and for ethically questionable financial transactions between the various organizations he controlled. In the end, Robertson's campaign for the presidency led to no other major victories. However, the campaign was still considered a success for the Christian Coalition because it energized members and built the organization from the ground up.

Political strategist Ralph Reed is credited with the success of this organization through the 1990s. There are two political tactics for which the Christian Coalition became well known. First, on the Sunday before major elections, churches all over the country distribute the Christian Coalition's voter guides during church services. These guides report candidates' views on issues of concern to the religious right. The Christian Coalition claims that the guides do not indicate any endorsement or opposition from them or from the churches distributing them. This is important because both the Christian Coalition and the churches are exempt from taxes by the IRS, but that exemption requires that they limit their political activity to education only. Christian Coalition opponents claim that these voter guides are not at all non-partisan guides, but that they are specifically designed to help Republicans and hurt Democrats. So far, though, the IRS has not revoked the Christian Coalition's tax exempt status.

Second, the organization supports candidates who run for office without making their allegiance to the Christian Coalition public. Often in smaller local races for school board and city council, the Christian Coalition has successfully helped candidates across the country to be elected in this manner.

Both tactics have been viciously criticized by the Coalition's opponents, but the Coalition's supporters have praised them as highly effective.

By the 2000 election the Christian Coalition had lost many of its central staff members, including Reed himself, and the organization did not seem to play a significant role in that election. However, the Christian right has shown a remarkable ability to restructure themselves, and thus far each time it seems that their influence has lagged, they have made a comeback.

The Evangelical Left

Most people identify Evangelicalism with political conservatism in America. While this is a reasonable generalization, it is also true that there is another dimension to Evangelicalism and politics: the Evangelical Left. Often identified with Jim Wallis, Ron Sider, and *Sojourners* magazine, the movement has its roots in the early1970s. These Christians, who embrace conservative Christian theology and biblical interpretation, developed a lengthy agenda of liberal political causes. They are pacifist, meaning they oppose war in general and nuclear weapons in particular. They promote concern for the environment as an issue of Christian concern, referring to the passage in the book of Genesis where God made Adam and Eve responsible to care for the earth. They advocate racial justice and reconciliation, and seek to work on what they see as the root causes of poverty. For them this often includes giving up material possessions and living in poor communities as part of those communities. They support equality between men and women in marriage, society, and the church by advocating Christian Feminism.

6

Important American Evangelical Leaders

FROM ITS EARLIEST DAYS IN AMERICA, THE EVANGELICAL PROTESTANT community has looked most often to the pulpit for leadership. Starting as preachers, many Evangelical leaders moved on to have great influence, as we have seen, in politics, culture, and society. Their faith leads them to these positions of responsibility, while their unique talents elevate them above other, similar religious leaders. Here are short biographies of some of the most influential Evangelical religious leaders in American history.

Dwight L. Moody (1837–1899)

Dwight L. Moody was raised in a small town in New England. He built a small shoe business into a success in Chicago and then drew on his business skills to build an evangelistic empire. His partner, musician Ira Sankey, has given music a central place in religion, writing more than 1,200 hymns that are still sung in churches today.

In 1873, Moody and Sankey went to Great Britain on a preaching tour that was so well received that it lasted for two years. They then returned to America, where they lived and preached in American cities for the rest of their lives.

Moody downplayed doctrinal issues because he considered them to be divisive. To him, the Gospel was straightforward and could be understood

Moody Goes to School

Dwight Moody is largely credited with being the father of the Bible School Movement. In 1886 Moody established what would become the best-known of the Bible institutes, Moody Bible Institute in Chicago. He believed strongly in the ability of education to promote godliness which would, in turn, result in social change. The Institute's *Moody Monthly* is still one of the most widely recognized fundamentalist publications, and Moody Press is one of the most important conservative Christian publishing houses.

Moody was convinced that the world quickly needed Christians willing to dedicate their lives to preaching the Gospel. "Gap men" he called them, meaning they should stand in the gap between the present time and the quickly approaching return of Jesus. As part of this commitment, he convened student mission conferences in his home state of Massachusetts. These conferences were well-attended and students then returned to their own campuses, energized for ministry.

PRECEDING PAGE
Pastor to presidents
Although slowed in recent years by ill health, Billy Graham maintains his national influence as a minister. He has prayed and consulted with presidents since the 1950s.

and accepted by everyone. Theological debates over issues like predestination and free will were nothing more than distractions from the simple truth he called the three Rs: ruin by sin, redemption by Christ, and regeneration by the Holy Spirit.

But some aspects of the end times theology of evangelical Christianity did play a central role in Moody's theology and in his preaching. He was known to say that God had given him a lifeboat and told him "save all you can." Like the successful evangelists before him, and like many of those who would follow him, Moody was known for his simple, direct messages put forth in memorable language.

Frances Willard (1839–1898)

The 19th century marked significant changes in the roles open to women, and no one exemplified those changes more than Frances Willard. Born near Rochester, New York, she moved with her strict Methodist family to Ohio and then Wisconsin. Willard never seemed to have embraced the traditional limitations placed on women. She attended schools in Wisconsin and Illinois and graduated in 1859, after which she became a teacher and a secretary to the Methodist Centenary Fund. This job gave her opportunities to travel in Europe and the Middle East, a level of mobility unheard of for women at the time.

She became president of Evanston College for Women, vice president of the Association for the Advancement of Women and, ultimately, led the Women's Christian Temperance Union (WCTU). Under Willard's leadership the WCTU fought for the prohibition of alcohol (see page 68), but also fought for women's rights, including the right to vote, protection of children, and labor rights.

Willard did not argue for women's rights based on the equality of men and women, and to those of us accustomed to such arguments her approach may seem odd. It was, however, in keeping with 19th-century views on gender. Then, men and women were sometimes believed to be completely different from one another, but women were thought to be more pure, spiritual, and holy than men. So much so, in fact, that they were charged with protecting the morality of the entire society because it was thought that men were largely incapable of doing so. Willard capitalized on this by arguing that women had to be given the right to vote in order to keep their God-given responsibility to protect home and society from evils such as alcohol.

For Willard, prohibition of alcohol was a women's rights issue. The Industrial Revolution had created poverty and hardship as people flooded the cities looking for work. In this context, alcohol became an escape, for some, from loneliness, despair, and disappointment. But such an escape came at a cost, especially to the women and children left at home when the men met at saloons and spent what little money there was on alcohol. The cost was sometimes even higher—in terms of domestic violence—when the drunken men returned home.

Like many of her day, Willard strongly believed that education would solve America's social problems. However, she went further than most: She also realized that opportunities for girls were even fewer than those for boys. She fought for kindergartens for girls and boys and industrial training for young women so that they would be able to support themselves, and wrote a book encouraging young girls to strive to achieve their potential, *How to Win: A Book for Girls.* Willard led the WCTU until her death in 1898.

Billy Sunday (1862–1935)

Born in Iowa in relative poverty, Billy Sunday gained fame as a major league baseball player and then later as the greatest of the revivalist showmen. No quality is more important to the success of the revivalist preacher than showmanship, and Sunday had plenty of it.

During eight years in baseball that brought Sunday from his rural home to America's cities, he learned about urban life in the

In another game
Outfielder Billy Sunday played for the Chicago Cubs and Pittsburgh Pirates in an eight-year professional baseball career. He went on to greater fame as an evangelist after leaving the game.

saloons and theaters. He drew on those experiences in his sermons for the rest of his life. He was converted in Chicago in 1886 when, after a night of drinking, he heard evangelists from the Pacific Garden Mission and was "born again." He continued playing baseball and volunteered at the YMCA, where he told inspirational stories to young men. When his baseball career ended in 1890, he joined the YMCA staff to teach "self improvement and Christian manhood."

In 1893 he joined the staff of a revivalist who taught him the "revivalist business." Although calling revivalism a business may seem somewhat cynical today, the end of the 19th century was a time of tremendous respect for business and business leaders. Sound business practices were considered the best practices by which to run a ministry and it was generally considered that the same qualities that would make one a business success would also make one a good Christian: hard work, persistence, determination, and focus. At this time, many considered success to be a result of godliness from which flowed a moral responsibility (and also the financial means) to help the less fortunate.

After working as an advance man in the revival business for two years (traveling ahead of the revival to drum up interest in the coming show), Sunday started out on his own in small towns. Within five years he was preaching his emotional message in his distinctive acrobatic style. Sunday would literally jump around the stage, falling, spinning, and flailing about. He would imitate drunks and theater-goers, to the amusement of his audiences. He was also known to jump up on the pulpit and wave his American flag. Sunday's form of patriotism was also in keeping with the times. Christians, both liberal and conservative, maintained ideas about America as God's chosen nation. It was seen as a religious and patriotic duty to spread American values and the American way of life around the world.

Like Moody before him, Sunday recognized the power of combining preaching and music. He worked for more than 20 years with Homer Rodeheaver (1880–1955), founder of Rainbow Records. Rodeheaver's recording credits are vast, and some of his records were sold in the Sears Roebuck catalog.

By 1910 Sunday's revival meetings had moved to the major cities. In the optimistic times before World War I and the social upheaval of the 1920s, Sunday saw conversion as the real answer to the problems posed by the urban environment—poverty, drunkenness, and indecency—and promoted his events as the most effective, efficient form of social reform.

Aimee Semple McPherson (1890–1944)

Aimee Elizabeth Kennedy was born to a farming family in Ontario, Canada. Her mother was a devout member of the Salvation Army, and Aimee's public speaking career began in her early childhood when she actively spoke out on temperance and other issues. Her speaking abilities won her medals from the Loyal Temperance Union, the children's organization affiliated with the WCTU.

In 1907, while attending Pentecostal meetings, she was exposed for the first time to end times theology and Christians who spoke in tongues. She also met evangelist Robert Semple, and the two fell in love. After burning her ragtime sheet music, novels, and dancing shoes, the two married in what must be considered an unconventional ceremony; their marriage vows included promises not to limit each other's work for the Lord. The couple went to China as missionaries, but Semple died a year later of dysentery and Aimee was left with a one-month old baby. Aimee Semple returned to the United States.

In 1912, she married Harold McPherson, taking his name as well. Never wavering in her devotion to the ministry, she only accepted his proposal when he agreed that he would not stand in the way of her preaching.

Aimee preached up and down the Atlantic Coast, holding revival meetings. She became known for her very theatrical preaching style; even her touring car had the words "Jesus is Coming Soon—Get Ready" on one side and "Where Will You Spend Eternity?" on the other side.

Sister Aimee
Passionate, popular, and controversial, Aimee Semple McPherson was one of the most famous evangelists in the country in the first decades of the 20th century.

In 1918, with her mother Minnie Kennedy as her business manager, she went to rapidly growing city of Los Angeles, and in 1921 she and Harold divorced. Sister Aimee, as she became known, was phenomenally successful in Los Angeles, and was especially known for her healing services. One of the earliest media evangelists, by 1922 she was developing a following for her radio preaching on what she called "the four-square Gospel." This meant that, according to Sister Aimee, other churches were preaching only part of the Gospel and were neglecting the gifts of the Spirit.

In 1923, she opened Angelus Temple in Los Angeles, and services there included speaking in tongues and miraculous healings. The building seats 5,300 people and was regularly filled to capacity when Sister Aimee was preaching. It was topped by a rotating, illuminated cross visible for 50 miles. She went on to found a Bible college called Lighthouse of International Foursquare Evangelism (L.I.F.E.) in 1925, which is still located in Los Angeles, and the International Church of the Foursquare Gospel in 1927. She established more than 400 branch churches, or "lighthouses," and sponsored 178 mission stations throughout the world. Throughout her lifetime she traveled to more than 250 foreign missions.

On May 18, 1926, she mysteriously disappeared while swimming in the Pacific Ocean, and was presumed dead. She then reappeared in June with a bizarre tale of being kidnapped and taken to Mexico. Coincidentally, Kenneth G. Ormiston, the engineer for her radio station, had not been seen during Aimee's absence—and many believed the two were having an affair.

This was not the only controversy in Sister Aimee's life, as her business activities as head of Angelus Temple resulted in numerous legal actions. She died from an accidental overdose of sleeping pills.

Billy Graham (b. 1918)

The influence of Billy Graham has extended far beyond the evangelical community. Born near Charlotte, North Carolina, the young Graham attended evangelical schools and became active in Youth for Christ. He first preached at a revival in Los Angeles in 1949, where he already showed the characteristic style that would mark his ministry. He was clear and direct, full of feeling, but not highly emotional as others had been; Graham is noted for his charisma, his humility, and his sincerity. Perhaps the quality most important to his success has been that he is perceived as an authentic, honest Christian man in a down-to-earth way that people find easy to relate to.

During the 1950s Graham's anti-communism made him popular and well respected. His association with President Richard M. Nixon's administration and the scandals that rocked it posed a challenge to Graham's respectability, but through it all Graham managed to maintain a position above the fray. Observers often comment that, although his ministry has spanned one decade after another in which the only constant influence was change, it is amazing how steadfast and unchanging his message has been.

It is said that more people around the world have seen Graham, thanks to his televised crusades, than any other human being in history. Graham has been a trusted advisor to American presidents from Harry Truman and Richard Nixon to Ronald Reagan and Bill Clinton.

His Billy Graham Evangelistic Association has been a major influence in the evangelical world through its support of such institutions as the magazine *Christianity Today*, the Fuller Theological Seminary, and Wheaton College, which now houses the Billy Graham Archives. At 84 years old in 2002, he suffers from occasional health problems but still leads an active public life.

Influence from Overseas

One of the influences on Martin Luther King's use of nonviolence and civil disobedience was Mahatma Gandhi (1869–1948), the leader of a movement that helped India win its independence from Great Britain in 1947. Gandhi was a Hindu, and from that faith he brought the concept of *ahimsa*, or nonviolence, to India's struggle. He developed such tactics as fasting and taught his followers not to react to violence with more violence.

King studied Gandhi's methods and even traveled to India to meet with people from Gandhi's movement. It was an important cross-religious connection in the history of the struggle for civil rights in America.

Martin Luther King, Jr. (1918–1968)

Martin Luther King, Jr. was born in Atlanta, Georgia, and became America's most important Evangelical civil rights leader. King balanced criticism of America and its policies on race with a vision that called on Americans to live up to their own values of freedom, justice, and equality. His "I Have a Dream" speech, given at the March on Washington in 1963, became the most well known of his speeches and, in many ways, encapsulated his vision.

King was raised in a black middle class family, which helped him escape some of the harshest realities of racism during his youth, and enabled him to develop a sense of hope and optimism about the future. He was also raised in the church, as he came from a long line of Baptist ministers. For King, like many African-American leaders, the church served as a training ground for leadership like no other.

Because of the King family's social status and economic means, young Martin was able to enroll in Morehouse College at the age of 15.

A King among men
Martin Luther King, Jr., was the most important civil rights leader in American history. He drew much of the inspiration for his fight for civil rights from his Baptist beliefs and ministry.

In his junior year he decided to become a minister and later attended Crozier Seminary, then Boston University, where he eventually earned his doctorate.

King's youth in the South was spent under segregation laws known as Jim Crow (see page 75). Black leaders who grew up in the officially unsegregated North argued that there were different forms of racism there, but King came to see integration as the key to achieving racial equality nationwide.

King first rose to prominence as a civil rights leader during the Montgomery, Alabama, bus boycott in 1955 (see page 75). The young King came to believe that nonviolent civil disobedience was the most effective tool against segregation. Sit-ins, boycotts and other protests were then organized to desegregate businesses and institutions all over the South.

Blacks and whites all over America came to see King as the central representative of this movement. He drew heavily from his Christian heritage, seeing the parallels between the suffering of the victims of racism and the suffering of Christ. In 1968, King was assassinated at the Lorraine Motel in Memphis, Tennessee. He was only 39 years old.

In some ways, King has become even more symbolically significant since that time. In addition to organizing and mobilizing African Americans, King called on white Americans to take seriously the American dream, to demand justice and equality for all Americans. King has become the symbolic representation of the commitment of Americans, black, white and brown, to do that.

EBENEZER BAPTIST CHURCH

Martin Luther King, Jr.'s church in Atlanta is a popular tourist attraction, hosting more than 600,000 visitors annually. Although the church, at 450 Auburn Avenue NE, no longer holds services, it does house offices and visitor facilities. In 2001, the National Park Service, which helps run the visitor center, announced a major renovation project that will help with the building's heating and plumbing systems as well as restore and beautify the entire church. Throughout this renovation, the church is open for visitors. Along with a trip to the MLK Memorial nearby, a visit to Ebenezer can help people feel a real connection to this important time in America's history.

Pat Robertson (b. 1930)

Marion G. "Pat" Robertson's family history is, indeed, impressive. His father was a U.S. Senator and he is a descendent of a signer of the Declaration of Independence. He was educated at the best schools in the country: Washington and Lee, Yale Law School, and then New York Theological Seminary.

As he tells the story, he and his wife were living the lives of New York socialites when, after failing the New York Bar exam at the age of 26, Robertson began to question the direction of his life. His interest in the ministry arose from a sense that he was not making much of a difference in the world. He began pastoring a small inner city church and in 1961 bought a small television station, which was the beginning of the Christian Broadcasting Network (CBN).

Five years later, as host of *The 700 Club* Robertson transformed religious programming. In fact, Robertson has often argued that he is not a televangelist, because *The 700 Club* is a Christian news and talk show, rather than a televised revival.

By 1977, Robertson's CBN broke new ground by using a satellite to broadcast its shows globally. Also in 1977, Robertson founded CBN University in Virginia Beach, Virginia. Now an established Christian university, CBN University has several graduate programs, including a strong media program and a law school.

In the late 1980s, Robertson was the target of much ridicule when he ran for president (see page 91). Like many Pentecostals, Robertson holds religious views that secular Americans often find difficult to understand; in his case, those views were readily available to his political opponents since he had written about them. Robertson claims to talk with God on a regular basis, and claims to receive some very explicit information from Him, such as when to buy TV stations and where to locate CBN. His presidential campaign was unsuccessful but led to the founding of the Christian Coalition in 1989 (see page 91).

Throughout the 1990s, the Christian Coalition under the direction of Ralph Reed became the most influential of the religious right political groups. In addition to the Coalition's activities in electoral and legislative politics, Robertson's empire also includes an organization to influence the legal system. American Center for Law and Justice (ACLJ), headed by Jay Sekulow, was founded by Robertson and is housed on the CBN University campus. ACLJ, in Robertson's words, is to be a Christian alternative to the American Civil Liberties Union. Much like ACLU, the ACLJ provides legal assistance in cases that have precedent-setting significance for issues related to religion. They have argued several church-state cases before the U.S. Supreme Court.

Robertson continues to influence American culture and politics through his vast empire of organizations.

Faith in the Oval Office

Since the election of President Jimmy Carter in 1976, almost every victorious American presidential candidate has laid claim to conservative Protestant faith. Carter, a Southern Baptist and the first president who claimed to be born again, was supported by many in the revivalist, Evangelical tradition and the denominations in which that tradition is represented.

Many conservative Christians thought that anyone who was a "born again Christian" would necessarily agree with them on political issues as well as theology. The Carter Presidency, though, taught them otherwise, as it was characterized by traditional Democratic policies that seemed, to the conservative Christians, to be downright liberal and unchristian.

Ronald Reagan, elected in 1980, seems to have been the most effective president at energizing conservative Christian voters—though ironically, he rarely attended church. He shared the conservative's political views on issues such as women's rights, abortion, evolution,

God and Sports

Athletes are among the most prominent people in America. In recent years, more and more of them have been more open about their faiths—none more so than the growing group of pro stars who are evangelical Christians. It is not unusual for players to meet on the field after a game for a group prayer. Bible study sessions are held regularly by players and their families. Many teams have a chaplain who works with players. Before every NASCAR (National Association for Stock Car Auto Racing) race, drivers can meet in a chapel service. The Fellowship of Christian Athletes works to spread the message of Gospel through athletic events, personal appearances, and other means.

The place of religion in sports is often hotly debated. Some fans are uncomfortable with hearing their heroes say, "God wanted us to win today." Other fans enjoy sharing a faith point of view with athletic stars.

Eleven-time Pro Bowl defensive end Reggie White (b.1961, pictured with fellow Christian athlete Cris Carter, right), who retired in 2000 after a 16-year National Football League career, is perhaps the most well-known of the athletes who preach their faith. An ordained Pentecostal minister, he was never shy during his playing days about his faith in God and its influence on his life. White told reporters that he prayed long and hard about all the decisions in his career, including the major one he made when he signed as a free agent with the Green Bay Packers in 1993.

While making news by helping the Packers win Super Bowl XXXI, White later also made headlines with remarks he made that seemed to be anti-gay. The controversy over not only what he said, but over his role as an athlete-preacher, focused attention on the growing influence of Evangelicals on pro sports.

For more information on Christian athletes, check out the web site www.thegoal.com, which includes lists of athletes by sport.

the Soviet Union, taxes, and education. Conservative Christians consistently supported President Reagan through both his terms.

George Bush Sr., an Episcopalian, also won election with the broad support of the religious right—though he had to move considerably in their direction between his first campaign in 1980 and his successful one in 1988.

Although Bill Clinton never enjoyed the support of the religious right, he was a church-going Baptist. He did draw on the Evangelical, revivalist tradition for legitimacy when, in the midst of the scandals that plagued his presidency, he sought to counsel of Billy Graham, the most widely known evangelist of the century.

Most recently, George W. Bush can be seen as a culmination of this history, as he is a "born again" Methodist with a Reagan-style public religion. He raised eyebrows when, during the presidential debates, he was asked who his heroes were and he answered "Jesus." He told a story in which he, as a young man, found himself in much trouble. Bush explains that his conversion led to his focus on his family, his abstinence from alcohol, and a general spiritual remaking. All of this was in keeping with the values of conservative Christians and helped lead to their widespread support of his candidacy and his presidency.

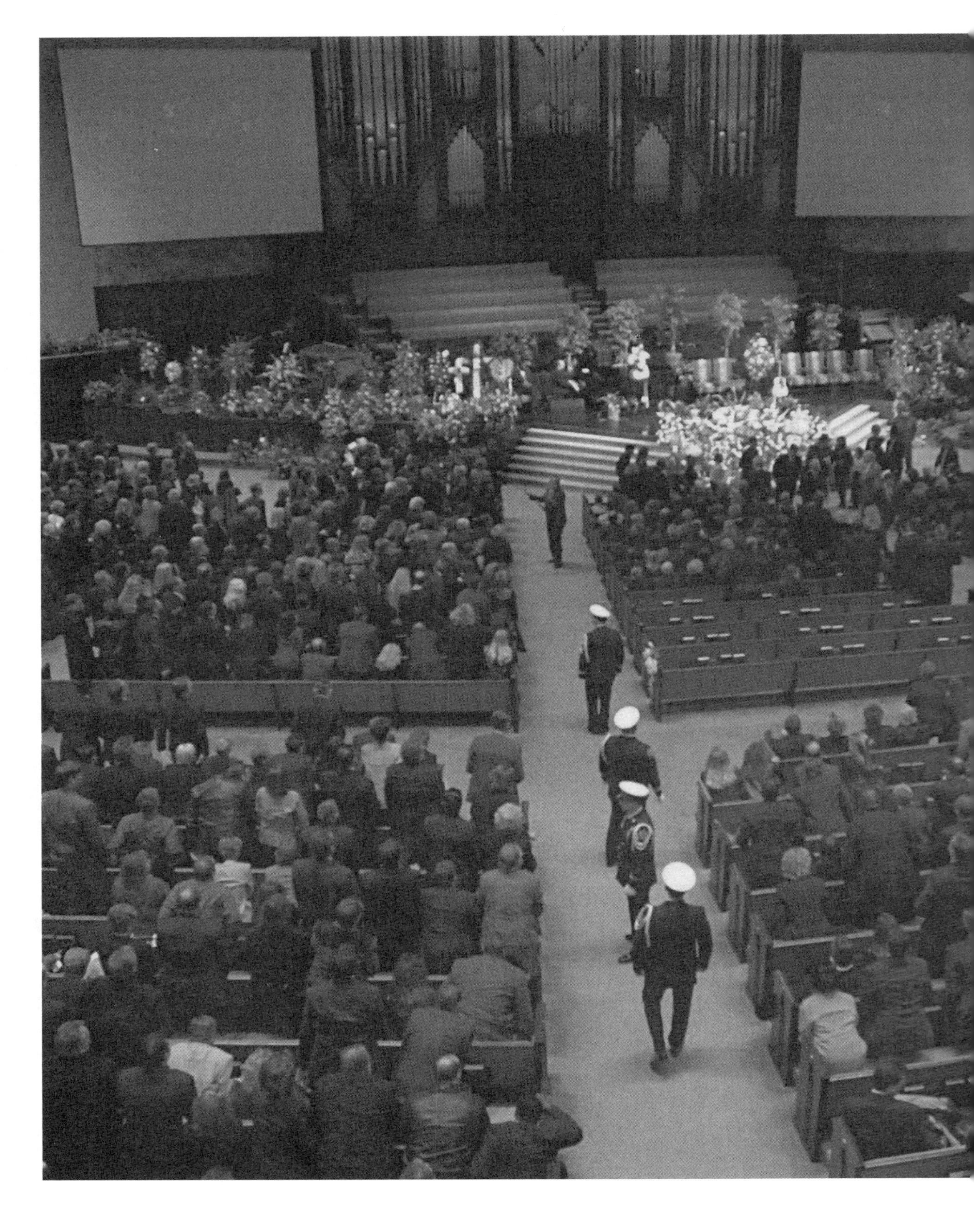

7

Evangelical Traditions Today and Tomorrow

THROUGHOUT THIS BOOK WE HAVE REFERRED TO THE SECULARIZATION process—the process by which religions become more worldly (secular), lose members, and are replaced by less worldly reform movements or new denominations that better meet the needs of common people. This process is very clear in the history of Baptists and Methodists. Both started out as growing denominations that connected with common people in simple, direct, ways, and they grew. Over time, the leaders of each of these denominations became more established, gaining wealth and education, and, then, in time, their numbers began to decline.

With Methodists we have seen a series of reform movements from Holiness to Pentecostalism, while "mainline" Methodism has declined. The story of the Baptists, however, is a bit different. Baptist leaders did indeed become more worldly and the "mainline" Baptist denominations have declined. But Southern Baptists have worked to turn back the tide of secularization. It is not clear whether they will be able to do so, but the story of their efforts will be important in the coming decades.

Southern Baptists Face the Future

In the last quarter of the 20th century, the Southern Baptist Convention faced a division that may ultimately lead the organization to divide between Fundamentalist and moderate factions.

In the late 1970s, a group of Fundamentalists within the Southern Baptist Convention came to the conclusion that liberals had taken control of several of the most important Baptist agencies and institutions, including the Southern Baptist institutions of higher education. These Fundamentalists thought that if they began electing sympathetic presidents, they could eventually control the various boards and effect a change for the better in the entire organization.

The division is between two groups that have fundamentally different ideas about what it means to be a Baptist. And in a sense, both sides are historically correct. One side looks to the earliest Baptists in the American colonies and says that to be a Baptist means to respect freedom of conscience, congregational autonomy, and the sanctity of the individual and his or her relationship with God. The other side points to the Baptist character that developed during the Fundamentalist-Modernist debates in which Fundamentalists believed that being a real Christian meant embracing a literalist view of the Bible.

PRECEDING PAGE
Big service for a big man
Calvary Chapel in Charlotte, North Carolina, was the scene of this 2001 service in memory of stock-car driver Dale Earnhardt, killed in a crash at the Daytona 500. Calvary churches are often distinguished by their large size and theatrical trappings.

The current controversy arose at the Southern Baptist Seminary in 1995. Amid a growing cry by conservatives for more control of the faculty and the curriculum, R. Albert Mohler was elected president of the school in 1993. In the next few years, he and others made women's ordination to the ministry a central issue at the seminary, moving the school's official position to the side of those who believed that the Bible, which they believe to be true and correct, does not allow women to be ministers.

Prospective faculty members are now required to articulate conservative views on four "issues of our day," three of which concern gender. These issues are abortion, homosexuality, women's ordination, and the uniqueness of the Gospel (that the only way to salvation is the acceptance of Jesus as savior.) This new requirement has made it increasingly difficult to hire qualified faculty and has produced a serious crisis at the Seminary.

Mohler says the issue of women's ordination is not new as a litmus test; in fact, he believes support for women's ordination was once an unspoken prerequisite for being hired at Southern. Now the tables are turned and Fundamentalists who control the Southern Baptist Convention and Southern Seminary have placed gender issues at cen-

Evangelical lightning rod
As president of the Southern Baptist Seminary, R. Albert Mohler has been at the center of several controversial policies and practices, including debate on the role of women in the ministry.

ter stage in their battles with moderates. The inerrancy of the Bible is no longer the central test of orthodoxy at Southern but has been replaced by opposition to women's ordination and gay rights.

This division is present in the denomination as a whole and is likely to continue to raise controversies. As discussed, the Southern Baptists are organized as a denomination only for the purpose of cooperating in projects such as missions and the production of Sunday School materials. The more moderate faction within the convention has withdrawn its financial support from some of those organizations and has begun alternative efforts. This action may foreshadow a bigger split.

New Ways of Looking at Things

As we move from the end of the 20th century to the beginning of the 21st, religion of feelings has become increasingly more popular than religion of reason. This is, perhaps, because our culture has come to see the limitations of science and rationality. The objective truths that religion was once thought to hold now seem more open to question; what we believe we know now seems more tentative than it might have in generations past.

Even conservative Christians are less likely to center their religious lives around debates over the correct reading of the book of Genesis, whether infants or adults should be baptized, and even the inerrancy of the Bible. Even those who hold strong views on these questions are more likely to recognize the possibility that they might be wrong. As a result, religious people are more likely to emphasize the personal dimensions of their faith. For instance, they might say, "I am not religious but I am very spiritual."

The Evangelical, Fundamentalist, Pentecostal, charismatic, and revivalist Christian world we have been exploring has responded to this change with what has been called "new paradigm churches." A paradigm is a way of looking at things, so this label is intended to convey that these churches are in some way distinctly different from the churches of the past. One way in which they are different is that they play down the theological issues that have divided these groups in the past. For example, they believe that the "gifts of the spirit" (speaking in tongues, etc.) can still be part of Christian life but they often argue that those gifts are not necessarily central to the life of the church.

Instead of beliefs being central to Christian life, for new paradigm Christians, the central part of Christian life is their relationship with Jesus, especially as it is expressed in relationships with other Christians. These churches have their origins in the Jesus Movement of the 1960s. Through the 1980s and 1990s the new paradigm churches worked to attract baby boomers, and in the 1990s many of them began restructuring themselves to attract the children of baby boomers, sometimes called Generation X. They now exist all over the world and are one of the most rapidly growing segments of Christianity. We will look at three examples of new paradigm churches and then explore some of the characteristics they share.

Calvary Chapel

At the heart of the beginnings of the Jesus Movement is Chuck Smith's Calvary Chapel in Southern California. Calvary Chapel grew out of the International Church of Calvary Chapel, which grew out of the International Church of the Foursquare Gospel founded by Aimee Semple McPherson (see page 99). Chuck Smith (b. 1926) had attended L.I.F.E. Bible College and had become a Foursquare pastor. Over time, however, he grew dissatisfied and started his own church in Corona, California. His church was beginning to grow when, in 1965, he was asked to become the pastor of a very small nearby church called Calvary Chapel in the beach community of Costa Mesa.

Smith had a daughter in college at the time, and she knew some students who identified themselves as hippies. But these were hippies of a different sort because they were also born-again Christians. He began to ask to meet some of them and before long he was working to meet their needs and to bring Jesus to them and other hippies. Many of them had no place to live, so, in what became a relatively common practice in these churches, Smith invited them to live in his family's home. He and the church soon rented several houses for the growing community.

Many of these new Christians had had negative experiences with forms of Christianity based on following rigid rules, so they saw these communities as places to become disciples and learn to live an authentic Christian lives. The church grew rapidly and each time its members expanded their facilities more people arrived than there was room for. Within 10 years they were in a facility that would seat 3,000 people and were holding three services on Sunday mornings. The group spread and by 2000 there were more than 600 Calvary Chapels worldwide, ranging from small congregations that have just been formed to established ones with 7,000 members.

In keeping with their dislike for formal structures, Calvary congregations retain their independence. Calvary members do believe in the gifts of the spirit but practices such as speaking in tongues and miraculous healings are much more common at home churches and small group meetings than in the main church services. Bible study and music are the central parts of the main services. Smith is known for his distinctive style of teaching the Bible, taking the text, passage by passage, and exploring its meaning and significance.

Going out into the world
The Calvary Church, one of the new paradigm churches, also focuses on missionary work. This 1998 photo shows Joseph and Donna Huen, Calvary Missionaries in Nicaragua who have adopted 24 children into their family.

While the Jesus Movement has evolved into what are now called new paradigm churches, its influence is seen in many of the churches experiencing the most rapid growth today. It is perhaps ironic that a distinctive commitment of the Jesus Movement—that churches should be relevant to people's lives—ultimately meant that the movement itself could not stay the same.

Hope Chapel

Another of these new paradigm churches, Hope Chapel, is a fellowship movement within the Foursquare denomination. Hope Chapel founder Ralph Moore grew up in the Foursquare church and believes he was called to the ministry at the age of six. He attended L.I.F.E. Bible College in Los Angeles and became an assistant pastor, and in 1971, took the pastorate of a small church in Redondo Beach, California, which had only 75 members.

The climate in 1971 was somewhat different from the climate faced by Chuck Smith a few years earlier. The hippie movement had passed, but Moore decided that the group he needed to address was young, single adults. Members of his church distributed copies of David Wilkerson's book *The Cross and the Switchblade* (published in 1990), which detailed Wilkerson's journey out of the drug culture, among the youth frequenting the beaches of the area. They purchased an empty bowling alley in Hermosa Beach, and they now have 2,500 people attending weekend services from Friday through Sunday.

With more that 30 churches now affiliated with Hope, Moore pastors a new church in Hawaii, and the Hermosa Beach church is pastored by Zac Nazarian. All the Hope Chapels are actually Foursquare churches still, but with the growing membership in their fellowship, they have significant independence from the institutional demands of the denomination. Similar to Calvary Chapels, contemporary music is central to the life of the congregation. The gifts of the spirit are more in practice in the main services than at Calvary, and the biblical teaching style is much the same.

The Vineyard Movement

The third of the movements that make up the new paradigm churches is the Vineyard movement, begun in 1974 by Ken Gulliksen. Gulliksen had the experience of speaking in tongues at the age of 17. After a time in the military he joined Calvary Chapel, where he became a pastor, learned to teach in Smith's style and developed a vision for building churches. He started several Vineyard Churches that were associated with Calvary but differed from the other Calvary Chapels in terms of the emphasis placed on the gifts of the spirit.

At the same time, John Wimber (1924–1997), a professional musician, had become a Quaker, adopting the Quaker commitment to the poor. He began meeting with other Quakers in small groups, but as these groups began to emphasize the gifts of the spirit they grew away from the Quakers and met on their own in Yorba Linda, California. They soon associated with Calvary Chapels but, since Calvary Chapels played down the charismatic gifts, the association was less than perfect.

In 1982 Gulliksen's churches and Wimber's churches left Calvary in a friendly parting of the ways and formed the Vineyard movement as it exists today. The movement capitalized on Wimber's organizational skills and he became recognized as its leader. Gulliksen continues to do what he does best, which is to create new churches. There are now over 600 Vineyard Churches around the world, and in the late 1980s Vineyard formally declared itself a denomination. Wimber died in 1997, but the movement remains strong.

LAUGHING REVIVALS

In a somewhat ironic development, a recent series of revivals led to a split from Vineyard that mirrors the Vineyard's earlier split from Calvary. Originating in a Vineyard Church at the Toronto airport and then spreading to churches throughout the United States and the world, the Toronto Blessing, sometimes called the laughing revival, has been highly controversial. In addition to speaking in tongues and experiencing miraculous healings, those attending the laughing revivals have reported uncontrollable ecstatic laughter, paralysis, and many other responses to the perceived presence of the Holy Spirit. While many of these practices have been looked on with suspicion, each has precedence in earlier revivals dating back to the First Great Awakening in the 1700s.

New Church Characteristics

There are many similarities in the characteristics of these new paradigm churches. We have already explored contemporary Christian worship music, but its centrality in these churches cannot be overemphasized.

Many of the people who attend these churches do so because of the worship music. In fact, it is so central that the term "worship" actually refers specifically to the musical part of the service. In some other churches the central act of worship is thought to be the preaching of the Word, while in Catholic and Episcopal churches the central act of worship is communion.

The new paradigm churches are all somewhat anti-institutional. All are suspicious of denominations—some more so than others. All have their roots in the baby boomer criticisms of traditional religion and each avoids the trappings of religion. They are much more likely, for example to meet in a warehouse or a rented public school building than in anything we might recognize as a sanctuary.

Since these churches are specifically concerned with being culturally relevant, the character of them is often reflective of the communities in which they minister. People attending new paradigm churches in beach communities often come in T-shirts, shorts, and sandals, while those attending churches located in suburban areas (such as Willow Creek Community Church outside Chicago) often come in khakis and polo shirts and their facilities look like the corporate facilities where they spend their weekdays.

The backgrounds of those who minister in these churches typically also mirrors the background of the members. The congregations targeting youth movements and the drug culture often have ministers who have lived in that world themselves. Those drawing suburbanites often have backgrounds in the business world and some even hold MBAs (Masters of Business Administration) rather than MDivs (Masters of Divinity), the standard degree for ministers. Stained glass windows are typically absent. Ministers most commonly dress in casual street clothes; they rarely wear suits, though some do, and they almost never wear vestments or any other specifically religious clothing.

A Different Sort of Sunday

The church activities of the new paradigm churches are often different too. Whereas older Fundamentalist and Evangelical churches commonly hold two Sunday services and a Wednesday Bible study, new paradigm churches build a sense of community with what is called "niche ministry." Since they are often so large, these churches offer lots of small programs to make people feel connected to the church. They often have small group meetings (sometimes called home churches), but they also might have prayer breakfasts once a week, meetings for business people, mid-day meetings for stay-at-home moms, aerobics classes with Christian music, teen groups, young adult groups, singles groups, newly singles groups, and so on. Each of the ministries is targeting a group of people with a shared interest.

These churches originated with baby boomers and reflect many of the cultural concerns of baby boomers. Specifically the anti-institutionalism of the baby boomers has led these churches to be suspicious of formal organizational structures, and their dissatisfaction with institutional religion has led them to try to create churches that do not seem like churches. Baby boomers emphasize experience over rationalism but they understand experience mostly in terms of relationships and play down much of the traditional Christian emphasis on mysticism.

As the baby boomers had children of their own, and as these churches that were already committed to being culturally relevant, began to try to reach those children, they made more changes. Gen-X-ers as this generation is called, share some characteristics of their parents, they take some further than their parents did, and differ from their parents in important ways. Gen-X-ers generally share their parents' distrust of institutions and authorities. Those who are leaders among Gen-X-ers have generally found that authority comes only from authentically sharing their own experience, not from credentials or status.

Gen-X-ers are often critical of their baby boomer parents, who, they think, sold out their counter-culture values on the 1980s and 1990s. Many more Gen-X-ers grew up in families with working mothers and families ending in divorce than any generation before them. Many feel that their parents were too busy to be parents and report that, as a result, they seek a better balance between family, work, and spiritual demands. Few grew up in church contexts, so they do not have the suspicion of religion that their parents had and, in particular, Gen-X-ers seem to be drawn to the mystical side of religion that their parents avoided. As a result, Gen-X churches often look more like churches than baby boomer churches. All of these characteristics of Gen-X-ers will shape the character of religion in America in the coming decades.

HISPANIC PENTECOSTAL CHURCHES

A number of Pentecostal or Evangelical churches have large percentages of Hispanic members. Here are some of the most prominent that have churches throughout the United States:

- Concilio Olazabal de Iglesias Latino Americano
- Latin American Council of the Pentecostal Church of God
- La Luz del Mundo
- Soldiers of the Cross of Christ
- Igreja Universal do Reinos de Dios

New Immigrant Religions

One of the most important factors shaping the future of religious traditions in America is the changing ethnic character of the United States, largely due to immigration. A combination of factors since the mid-1960s, including changes in immigration laws, and wars and economic turmoil, especially in Latin America, has transformed America from a largely European Protestant nation to a diverse, pluralistic one.

While many in these immigrant groups have historically been Catholic, the largest growth segment of Protestantism is Latin American Pentecostalism. Today more than 10 percent of Latin Americans identify themselves as Protestant, most of those Pentecostal. These Pentecostal churches are, in many ways, similar to non-immigrant American Pentecostal and Charismatic churches. Their members tend to be relatively young, the churches make use of contemporary Christian music (often Latino contemporary music), they practice the gifts of the spirit, and they tend to experience rapid growth.

The story of new immigrant Pentecostals also gives us an opportunity to look briefly at the character of immigrant religion in general. It is often the case that immigrants are more connected to religious communities once here than they ever were at home. Because the United States is a religiously diverse nation, immigrants can preserve the religious heritage from their home country, and thus preserve some of their culture, without complicating their adjustment to the new culture. This is often in contrast to the difficulties created when immigrants try to maintain their own culture by maintaining their language, for example.

There are other also reasons for a closer association with the church. Immigrant churches are often places to learn English and to adapt to the demands of American culture. They are places to make contacts for jobs, housing, and social services. And they serve as a familiar refuge from an overwhelming and unfamiliar new home.

Conclusion

Sociologists once thought that religions were strongest in places that had only one religious option. They thought that pluralism would raise questions that would weaken religion. It is interesting, though, that America, one of the first nations to embrace the separation of church and state and religious pluralism, is perhaps the most religious of modern nations. It seems that pluralism and freedom of religion make for very strong religions.

We have discussed how the mainline church radio programs lost out to Fundamentalist ones because the mainline programs were given free airtime and did not have to compete. In many ways this is an illustration of the whole process. In the context of religious freedom, religious communities have to compete with one another for members. This forces them to pay close attention to the needs and wants of potential members. This, in turn, makes them more appealing and causes them to grow. Religious communities that have a secure base of guaranteed support become unresponsive to potential members, and decline in numbers.

If, as we have suggested, the secularization process produces new, more vital, religious groups as older ones become more worldly, there is every reason to expect the revivalist, Evangelical religions in America to continue to grow and to change. In fact, in many ways it is better suited to doing so than other forms of American religion, because it embraces innovation as an effective way to reach potential converts, and it is especially suited to benefit from the growing emphasis on religion as a part of a person's individual experience.

Glossary

abolition the complete removal of something, in this case of slavery in the United States. From this came the name of the abolitionist movement, dedicated to eliminating slavery.

anabaptist literally meaning "rebaptizer," the name given to those who opposed infant baptism, claiming that only those who were old enough to make a profession of faith should be baptized.

Antichrist the identity of this person or entity is greatly debated, but one definition is found in *Webster's Dictionary,* 10th edition: "a great antagonist expected to fill the world with wickedness but to be conquered forever by Christ at his second coming."

Apocalypse the formal name for the Biblical book of Revelation. This term is also used to describe views about the end of the world that end in a great cataclysm.

Armageddon this term has many different meanings, but a general meaning would include a battle between the forces of good and evil at the end of the world.

Arminianism the theological tradition deriving from Jacobus Arminius, Dutch theologian and opponent of John Calvin in the Protestant Reformation. Arminianism emphasized freedom of will over the predestination of Calvinism.

baptism the Christian ritual that includes immersing the believer in water or sprinkling or pouring water on the believer's head. This symbolizes the believer being washed of sin. Different Christian denominations have disagreed over the appropriate method of performing this ritual, as well as over whether infants or only adult believers should be baptized.

Bible Belt the region of the United States most influenced by the second Great Awakening (c. 1797) and thereby most influenced by Baptist and Methodist denominations today. Mostly the southeastern part of the United States.

Biblical inerrancy the view that the Bible, at least in its original texts, is without error. This view became a test of orthodoxy among revivalist Christians during the early part of the 20th century and remains so in many parts of conservative Christianity today.

Biblical literalism From the beginning of the 20th century through today, this is a revivalist Christian claim to take the Bible literally.

born again term used by conservative Christians to refer to someone who has had a conversion experience in which they come to identify themselves fully as a Christian.

calling the notion, grounded in the work of John Calvin, that one's life work is service to God even if one is not a church leader or minister. Calvinists, and many conservative Christians, believe that all Christians have a calling.

Calvinism the theological tradition developed by John Calvin, brought to American by the Puritans. Calvinism emphasizes the impassable gulf between fallen humans and an all-powerful God. The doctrine of predestination (that God determined what each of us would do from the beginning of time) is central to Calvinism.

camp meeting originally the revivals held outdoors at Cane Ridge, Kentucky, but more recently any outdoor revival. The meetings, essential for the development of the Holiness movement, were initially loosely organized alternatives to regular church services.

episcopal a denomination that has bishops.

Episcopal belonging to the American wing of the Anglican Church (Church of England).

Evangelical literally referring to the Greek word for "the good news," this word can refer to a tradition that emphasizes evangelizing (that is, preaching the Gospel or proselytizing) or is broadly part of the Evangelical movement that has its roots in American revivalism.

evangelism the practice of seeking converts, sometimes also called proselytizing.

Fundamentalism the movement that derived from the series of books called *The Fundamentals* published in the early 20th century. This word is also often used to refer to the most conservative wing of any religion, which emphasizes the fundamentals of that religion.

free-church the more radical of the Reformation traditions that established themselves as separate from state churches.

Judgment Day the day during the end of the world when God will judge all people.

Kingdom of God Christians generally believe that there is a reality in which God reigns over history. They disagree over what this means. Some believe that the Kingdom of God is a heavenly, spiritual reality, others believe it is a historical reality that develops as Christianity influences the world, and still others (including many Baptists and Methodists) believe this refers to a literal 1,000-year reign of Jesus that follows the defeat of Satan.

gifts of the Spirit the New Testament, in particular in Paul's letters to the Corinthians, discusses gifts of the Holy Spirit given to Christians at Pentecost. Christians have different interpretations as to what the gifts mean, but they include speaking in tongues, miraculous healing, and prophecy. These texts provide the basis for the Pentecostal and Charismatic traditions.

grace Christians all believe that salvation comes through grace, the gift of a loving God. They disagree, however, over the means by which humans receive that grace. Sacramental Christians such as Catholics believe that God gives people grace through the sacraments (communion, baptism, marriage, etc.). Arminians believe grace is available to all who choose to accept it, while Calvinists believe that God chooses who will be saved and offers grace only to them.

new paradigm church churches rooted in the Jesus Movement of the 1960s that now target their ministries to baby-boomers, Generation-Xers, and more recently, the children of members of those generations. New paradigm churches emphasize relationships over doctrine, powerful worship through contemporary music, and making faith relevant to daily life.

Pentecost the holy day five days after Christ's ascension to heaven in the New Testament. The Bible says at Pentecost God sent his Holy Spirit to dwell among the people. All Christians celebrate this, but it is at the heart of the tradition known as Pentecostalism, which emphasizes miraculous gifts of the Holy Spirit.

Pietist Pietists emphasize the need for religious conversion followed by a life of piety or devotion, over doctrine. It has been one of the most significant themes in revivalist Protestantism.

premillennial dispensationalism the belief that at the end of time God will choose those who will survive and enter heaven.

presbyterian a denomination having an organization structure called a presbytery—a form of representational leadership

Presbyterian belonging to the denomination by that name.

Rapture the teaching among premillennial dispensationalists that Jesus will sweep believers up to spare them from living through some or all of the Great Tribulation.

Reformation the period (c. 16th century) during which various state churches in Europe broke from Roman Catholicism, forming what are now called Protestant denominations.

revival meeting a gathering at which evangelists attempt to lead people to conversion or at which the faithful gather to celebrate and renew their commitments.

TIME LINE

1620	Puritans arrive in Plymouth and establish the Massachusetts Bay Colony.
1730s	The First Great Awakening stimulates interest in the newer American-based Protestant churches.
1780s	Methodism is established in the United States.
1797	The Second Great Awakening continues work by preachers to convert many to a renewed spiritual devotion to Protestant Christianity.
1843	The Great Disappointment, when the end of the world predicted by George Miller does not occur.
1845	The Southern Baptist Convention is founded.
1893	C.H. Mason forms the Church of God in Christ, a Pentecostal church made mostly of African Americans.
1901	The Azusa Street Revivals in Los Angeles create the Pentecostal and Holiness movements.
1910	*The Fundamentals* are first published.
1925	The Scopes Monkey Trial focuses national attention on the debate between creationists and evolutionists, as well as the growing influence of Fundamentalists.
1965	Calvary Chapel is formed, part of growing Jesus Movement that would lead to creation of new paradigm churches.
1973	The U.S. Supreme Court issues the *Roe v. Wade* decision legalizing abortion, leading to the creation of the Christian-led Right-to-Life movement.
1980	Ronald Reagan is elected president and the political power of conservative Christians rises dramatically.
1987	Scandal brings down televangelist Jim Bakker.
1988	Another scandal affects televangelist Jimmy Swaggart.
2002	President George W. Bush signs an executive order allowing faith-based aid organizations to receive government funds.

RESOURCES

Reading List

Ammerman, Nancy Tatom. *Bible Believers: Fundamentalists in the Modern World.* New Brunswick, N.J.: Rutgers University Press, 1988.

Balmer, Randall. *Mine Eyes Have Seen the Glory.* New York: Oxford University Press, 1989.

Brown, Stephen F., *Protestantism (World Religions Series), revised edition.* New York: Facts On File, 2002.

Cimino, Richard and Don Lattin. *Shopping for Faith: American Religion in the New Millennium.* San Francisco: Jossey Bass Publishers, 1998.

Finke, Roger and Rodney Stark. *The Churching Of America 1776-1990.* New Brunswick, N.J.: Rutgers University Press, 1992.

Roof, Wade Clark. *A Generation of Seekers.* San Francisco: Harper San Francisco: 1994.

Resources on the Web

Southern Baptists
www.sbc.net
The official site of the Southern Baptist Convention, the largest Baptist organization in the United States. The site includes a directory of churches, as well as statement of the group's beliefs.

United Methodists
www.umc.org
The official site of the United Methodist Church, one of the largest Methodist organizations. Contains a directory and news of its programs and message.

Pentecostal site
www.iphc.org
A site run by the International Pentecostal Holiness Church, one of the oldest and largest Pentecostal organizations. Read about its different ministries and visit the history and belief sections to find out more.

Campus Crusade
www.billbright.com
Home site of the founder of the Campus Crusade for Christ, a national organization of students on college and high school campuses.

Here are the web sites of some of the other major Baptist or Methodist church organizations in the United States:

African Methodist Episcopal Church
www.amecnet.org

African Methodist Episcopal Zion Church
www.theamezionchurch.org

American Baptist Churches in the USA
www.abc-usa.org

Assemblies of God
www.ag.org/top

Christian Methodist Episcopal Church
www.cmesonline.org

Church of God (Cleveland, Tennessee)
www.churchofgod.cc

Church of the Nazarene
www.nazarene.org

National Baptist Convention, U.S.A.
www.nationalbaptist.com

Index

Note: *Italic* page numbers refer to illustrations.